Piety and Piracy

The History of Wapping and St Katharine's

by

Madge Darby

Published by The History of Wapping Trust - Charity No 290087
Book © The History of Wapping Trust 2011
Text © Madge Darby 2011

ISBN 978-1-873086-06-3

Acknowledgements

Original Text - Madge Darby

Design and Layout - John Tarby

Additional Research - Ray Newton

Captain Cook Research - Julia Rae

Proofreading - Helen Keep

Printing - Aldgate Press

Picture credits:

History of Wapping Trust

Tower Hamlets Local History Library

Museum in Docklands

Museum of London

Port of London Authority collection

John Tarby collection

Ray Newton collection

Steve Kentfield postcard collection

Paul Trevor collection

Supported by:

Rotary Club of Canary Wharf

Turks Head Trust

Front Cover - *"Molten Thames"* - www.claudeschneider.com
Back Cover - London Docks 1834

Table of Contents

St. Katharine's Dock, Wapping, in the early 21st Century - photo : John Tarby

Impression of Londinium AD60 from north west - site of Wapping downstream (top left)

Wapping's history has always been shaped by its geographical position, immediately to the east of the City of London.

Before any houses were built the Thames flowed through marshland, with a gravel shelf above it. On the north side the firmer ground came down to the water for about a mile. The site had other advantages. The river became narrow enough for a crossing and the water was fresh at all tides.

These factors made the site a natural place for a settlement and one probably existed at least from Celtic times. Legend says that London was named after King Lud; but a more prosaic expert opinion traces the name to the Celtic words for *"pool"* and *"hill"*.

After the Romans had invaded Britain in the first century AD, they transformed the Celtic village into the town of Londinium and made it an international port. The Roman historian Tacitus wrote that it was:

> *"...much frequented by many merchants and trading vessels"*

The town was laid out on the usual Roman plan and surrounded by walls. On the East the wall ran through the present site of the Tower of London, where its line can be seen, with a remaining fragment of wall higher up near Tower Hill Station.

Roman bath house in Wapping Lane

The Romans built roads, with one running along the gravel shelf to the East, approximately on the line of the Ratcliffe Highway, to a point where the gravel shelf again touched the river, at what later became Ratcliffe Cross. The remains of a Roman settlement have been found at the top of what is now Wapping Lane, with a stone bath house and wooden houses, possibly forming part of a Roman inn. They appear to date between 260 - 375AD.

The remains have been found of another Roman settlement at Ratcliffe Cross, where use was probably made of the natural landing place.

Roman remains in Wapping Lane

To the south of the Roman road the marsh protruded through a bend in the river, forming the area that was to become Wapping. What the Romans made of it we do not know. It would have been valuable land, so they may have built an earthwork wall to reclaim it from the marsh, but if so nothing of their work remains, in written records nor archaeological remains.

The earliest evidence of Wapping's origin lies in its name.

By the fifth century the Roman Empire was disintegrating from
conflicts within and under attack from the barbarians without and
the Roman legions were withdrawn from Britain.

The Romano-Britons who had lived under their protection were
further weakened by a great plague, in which, according to the
historian Gildas, so many died that the living were not able to
bury them.

The country was invaded by tribes from northern Europe, mostly
Angles and Saxons, who drove most of the survivors into the
remoter parts of the country. The name Wapping is of Saxon
origin, and evidence of its existence at this period.

The invaders had a different life-style from the Romans, who had
regarded town-life as the essence of civilisation. The Saxons were
country dwellers. They looted the Roman towns, but then left
them in ruins, shunning them as haunted.

Unlike the Romans, who had been converted to Christianity, the
newcomers were pagans.

The Saxons lived in
communities based on
kinship, which in the early
days were extended families,
and farmed their land in
common under a chief, who
was head of the family. They
lived in clusters of small huts
with a barn-like hall, which
was the home of the chief.

Modern reconstruction of a Saxon village

Many of the villages established at this time have names ending in
"ing", which in early English meant son. In place names it was a
contraction of the plural, *"ingas"*, meaning sons, or family. It was
often attached to the name of the chief to form the place name.

The English Place-Name Society conclude that Wapping is a name of this type, named after a chief called Waeppa, and that the name, originally Waeppingas, means *"the people of Waeppa"*.

Another community formed the original village of Stepney. This name appears first as Stebenhithe, meaning Staebba, or Stephen's landing place. This suggests that they took over the landing place of the Roman settlement at Ratcliffe Cross, but built their village further inland for greater safety from pirates.

Waeppa and his people have left no clue but their name to the life they led. They probably settled on one of the gravel outcrops near the marsh. They very likely moored their boats in the tidal creeks of the marsh and lived, as many of their successors were to do, from the river, fishing and trading with other settlements.

Londinium was in ruins and deserted. There is no evidence of continuous occupation through this period.

Waeppa and his people may have ventured over the derelict walls into the ruined town to find objects they could use or trade with, but they did not stay in the town, which was regarded with awe and fear as a place of disease and decay, lived in by ghosts.

Waeppa? - a 7th century Anglo Saxon chief

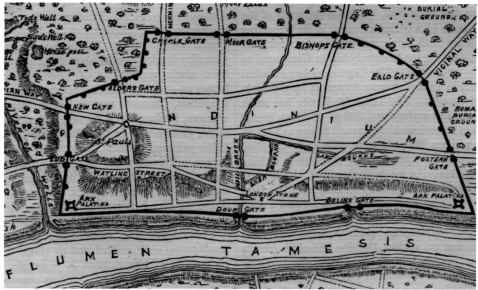

Victorian map of Medieval London

By the seventh century London had once more become a centre of trade, under the East Saxons. The Venerable Bede wrote:

> *"Their metropolis is the City of Lundonia, which is placed on the bank of that river, and is the mart of many nations resorting to it by land and sea."*

Ethelbert, King of Kent, had been converted to Christianity by St Augustine in 597. Sebert, the King of the East Saxons, was his nephew and was also converted. Bede recorded:

> *"King Ethelburt built the church of St Paul in the City of Lundonia."*

In the following years England was reconverted to Christianity. One of those who converted the South was St Chad, and local legend has always held that Shadwell was named after a well discovered by St Chad who gave it healing powers and that the name means St Chad's Well; but the experts, prosaic as ever, trace it to a well in a stream running through the marsh called the Shadfleet, or shallow river.

At the end of the eighth century there began a new series of

9

Alfred the Great

invasions, from Denmark, by the Vikings. London was sacked by the Vikings in 839.

English resistance became focused under Alfred, the King of Wessex, who had London rebuilt in 886. London was not the capital; that remained at Winchester. Under Alfred's leadership the advance of the Danes was halted and he became *"England's King and England's darling."*

In the next century, Alfred's great-grandson, Edgar, established his rule over all England and was recognised as overlord of Great Britain by the Kings of Scotland and Wales.

Edgar's reign was a time of peace and prosperity and London once more became a thriving town. Trade was re-established and foreigners came to England in peace, attracted by the culture and learning which flourished there.

The country was divided into hundreds, which in theory consisted of a hundred families, and Edgar enacted laws which laid down that each hundred was to elect twelve men to administer justice and ensure that the law was kept. Wapping was in the hundred of Ossulstone.

By then the social order had become more complex, with nobles, called eorls, at one end of the scale and ceorls, who tilled the land, at the other, paying for their land with goods or services.

"Cnihten Gild" plaque at St Botolph's, Aldgate

The first record of a grant of land in the Wapping area refers to this period, when King Edgar granted the land to the east of London's wall to a Guild of Knights, known as the Knighten Guild.

Their land stretched from the wall to a road running beside a stream through the marsh. The road was known as Nightingale Lane, a corruption of Knighten Guild, and retained this name for a thousand years until 1939, when the London

County Council changed it to Thomas More Street.

John Stow, the sixteenth century historian, recorded:

> *"There were thirteene Knights, or Soldiers welbeloved to the king and realme, for service by them done, which requested to have a certaine portion of land on the East part of the Citie, left desolate and forsaken by the inhabitants, by reason of too much servitude. They besought the king to have this land, with the libertie of a Guilde for ever: the king granted to their request with conditions following: that is, that each one of them should victoriously accomplish three combates, one above the ground one underground, and the third in the water, and after this at a certaine day in East Smithfield, they should run with Speares against all conmers, all of which was gloriously performed: and the same day the King named it knighten Guild, and so bounded it, from Ealdgate to the place where the bars now are toward the east, on both sides of the streete, and extended it towards Bishopsgate in the North...And againe towardes the South unto the river of Thames, and so farre into the water, as a horseman, entering the same, may ride at a low water, and throw his speare."*

Most guilds at this period were *"frith"* or peace guilds, set up for mutual security, and it is likely that the Guild of Knights undertook the defence of the eastern side of London. The services required for holding the land probably included the repair of the wall, which was heavy work and may have led to the previous inhabitants moving away. The bars were at Brick Lane in Stow's time.

Edgar's chief minister was Dunstan, who was Bishop of London from 959 to 961, when he became Archbishop of Canterbury.

While Bishop of London he held the land which formed the Manor of Stepney, which was later recorded as having belonged to the bishopric *"from time immemorial"*.

There was a wooden church in Stepney, dedicated to All Saints; but Dunstan is credited with having begun the building of the first stone church there. After he had died and been canonised the church was re-dedicated to St Dunstan and All

St Dunstan's, Stepney

11

St Dunstan's rood stone

Saints. Wapping was in its parish for seven hundred years.

The present building of St Dunstan's dates from the fifteenth century but it still has a rood stone dating from Saxon times.

After Edgar's death England soon ceased to be peaceful. In the reign of his son, Ethelred, known as the Reedless (ill-advised), or Unready, there was another invasion, by the Vikings. Canute the Dane sailed up the Thames, past Wapping, to London with 120 ships. The attack was repelled but Canute became King in 1016.

In 1042 the English monarchy was restored when Edgar's grandson, Edward the Confessor, became King.

Edward granted a Charter to the Guild of Knights, as Stow explained:

> *"These knightes had as then none other Charter by all the dayes of Edgar, Ethelred, and Cnutus, until the time of Edward the Confessor, whom the heires of those knights humblie besought to continue their liberties, whereunto he graciously graunting, gave them a deede thereof, as appeareth in the booke of the late house of the holy Trinitie. The said Charter is faire written in the Saxon letter and tongue."*

Part of Nightingale Lane in the 1930s

12

Artist's impression of The White Tower c1100

After his victory at the Battle of Hastings in 1066, William the Conqueror entered London and established a power-base there which led to it becoming the nation's capital.

In order to over-awe the citizens, William decided to build a fortress on the east side. The first building was a wooden fort, but in 1078 he had work started on a massive stone building, just inside the wall. He did not live to complete the building; that was done by his son, William Rufus, who saw the completion of the great stone keep which became known as the White Tower.

The wall served as an eastern defence, with one of its bastions later becoming the Wardrobe Tower. On the other sides the fortress was defended by an earthwork wall.

The building of this great fortress had its effect on the people living on the other side of the wall. It brought the centre of power nearer to them. The immediate effect was onerous, since much of the work of building the Tower fell on them. Later the duty of providing a watch or guard for the Tower fell on the people of the Tower Hamlets, which were villages within the parish of Stepney and included Wapping, Shadwell and Ratcliffe.

13

The Domesday Book

William the Conqueror made large grants of land to his followers and a more formal feudal system was established, under which the manor became the unit of local government outside the towns.

In 1084, when he needed money to finance the defence of the country against the Danes, William made a survey of the country, known as the Domesday Survey.

Wapping was not mentioned individually, but came under the Manor of Stepney, which was still held by the Bishop of London. The Domesday Book records:

"In Ossulstone Hundred the Bishop of London holds Stibenhede for 32 hides. There is land for 25 ploughs. To the demesne belong 14 hides and there are 3 ploughs, and among the villeins 22 ploughs. There are 4 mills rendering £4 16s less 4d. There is meadow for 25 ploughteams, pasture for the cattle of the vil and yielding 15s. woodland for 500 pigs and yielding 40s. The whole is worth £48...TRE £50. This manor belonged and belongs to the bishopric."

TRE (Tempore Regis Edwardi) was the value in the time of Edward the Confessor. A hide was about 120 acres, which was estimated to be the amount of land needed to support a household.

The villeins were bondmen. They held small-holdings which they farmed to support their families but in addition, they had to work for the lord of the manor on his demesne lands, that is the lands he retained himself. The villeins could not be compelled to perform services other than those laid down for their holdings, but they were not free to leave their land except by the permission of the lord of the manor.

After the death of William Rufus, who was accidentally killed by an arrow while hunting in the New Forest, the Conqueror's youngest son became king as Henry I.

Henry I was born in England and married a Scottish princess named Eadgyth, who was *"of than rihtan Ængla landes kyne kynne"* (of England's rightful royal line). Her parents were Malcolm King of Scots, who defeated Macbeth, and his wife, St Margaret of Scotland. Margaret was the sister of Edgar the Ethling, who was proclaimed King after the Battle of Hastings. They had to flee to Scotland after the Norman conquest. Eadgyth changed her name to Matilda.

Henry I

In 1108 Matilda founded the Priory of the Holy Trinity at Aldgate, to provide hospitality for travellers arriving in London. It was just inside the gate and was run by Augustinian canons, known as the black canons from their black habit.

Henry I confirmed the Charter of the Guild of Knights, but in 1125 they were persuaded to hand over their lands to the Priory, as Stow recorded:

> *"The Queene was a mean also that the land and English Knighten Guild was given unto the Prior Norman...the multitude of brethren praysing God day and night therein, in short time so increased, that all the Citie was delighted in the beholding of them: insomuch that in the yeare 1115 certaine Burgesses of London, of the progenie of those Noble English knights...coming together into the Chapter house of the said Church of the holy Trinitie, gave to the same Church and Canons serving God therein, all the lands and soke called in English Knighten Guild, which lieth to the wall of the Citie, without the same gate, and stretcheth to the river of Thames..."*

St Katharine's Church in Wyngaerde's Panorama

In 1147 another Queen Matilda, the wife of King Stephen, leased from the Priory of the Holy Trinity part of the land formerly held by the Guild of Knights and on it founded what she called *"my hospital next to the Tower of London"*. She placed her hospital in the custody of the Priory.

Queen Matilda depicted with a charter

Matilda's hospital became known as the Royal Hospital of St Katharine and gave its name to that area of Wapping. St Katharine was not mentioned in Matilda's charter, but the dedication existed from an early date, probably from the beginning. It was based on the legend, very popular at the time, of St Katharine of Alexandria, who refused to marry the Emperor, and was tortured on a spiked wheel and martyred.

In the middle ages, hospitals were charitable institutions of any type, mostly for the old, the sick and orphan children.

Matilda's charter said her hospital was to:

"...maintain in the said Hospital in perpetuity thirteen poor persons for the salvation of the soul of my lord King Stephen and of mine and also for the salvation of our sons Eustace and William and of all our children."

The hospital was a religious house and its twin duties were to celebrate mass for the souls of those mentioned in the charter, and to look after the inmates. Matilda made the hospital a grant of £20 per year.

The house probably consisted of one building serving both as Church and hospital, with a large nave, where the inmates were accommodated, cut off by a screen from the chancel where the services were held.

The 13 poor inmates were soon divided into a Master, or Warden, three brethren, who were priests, three sisters, who were nuns, and six poor, usually old people who were looked after by them.

In the following period the Plantagenet kings strengthened the defences of the Tower of London by building curtain walls around the White Tower. In doing so they intruded upon the land of the hospital.

Interior of St Katherine's

Stow recorded:

"Recompence was often promised, but never performed."

The hospital also found itself in trouble with the Priory of the Holy Trinity. The Prior claimed that the hospital's discipline had become lax and he appointed one of his own canons as Master.

The brethren appealed to Queen Eleanor, the wife of Henry III, claiming that the black canons were wasting their property and allowing the hospital to fall into decay. In 1257 the Queen sent the Bishop of London to look into the dispute. The Prior told him:

"as to the appointment of one of their own body to the Mastership of St Katharine's, it was done to reform the Brethren, too frequently inebriated."

Henry III

The Bishop supported the brethren, however, and removed the Master. The Priory was then forced, under threat of the King's displeasure, to surrender all claim to the hospital. They appealed to the Pope, who protested, but in vain. The hospital was put under royal patronage.

Henry III died in 1272 and was succeeded by his son Edward I. In 1273 the hospital received a new charter from the Queen Dowager.

Queen Eleanor's charter was the first to include the dedication to St Katharine, although it already existed and was mentioned in the dispute with the Priory of the Holy Trinity.

The Queen reconstituted the hospital as a memorial to her husband. The charter said her grants were:

> *"for the salvation of the soul of the Lord Henry of famous memory, King of England and our lord, and of our soul, and of the souls of the kings and queens of England, our predessors and successors, and of our ancestors and friends."*

The hospital was to pray for the souls of all the Kings and Queens of England.

The charter provided for a Master, or Keeper, and *"three priest Brothers"* with 24 poor persons, including:

> *"six... poor scholars, who shall assist the chaplains in church at the divine services, when they can conveniently leave their studies, so that by their services and assistance they may more fully deserve to be supported, with frugality, from the alms of the Hospital."*

The *"poor scholars"* were clerks in minor orders and there appears to have been an intention that St Katharine's should become a centre of learning. Henry III had been interested in education and made grants for scholars at Oxford and Cambridge

Another innovation was that each year on the anniversary of the death of Henry III, a halfpenny was to be given to each of 1,000 poor persons outside the hospital, thus extending its work to the surrounding area.

Eleanor granted the hospital the income from three manors and land in East Smithfield.

Queen Eleanor's charter laid down that the patronage of the hospital should be held by the Queen Consort, who should continue to hold it if she outlived her husband. The right to appoint the Master, brethren, sisters, clerks and other inmates was reserved in perpetuity to *"every queen succeeding us"*.

12th Century charter confirming rights of St Katharine's

Artist's impression of Menagerie

In the Middle Ages, before steam power, natural forces such as wind and tide had to be used for energy and use was made of the Thames, with its two tides a day, to grind corn through tide-mills along the banks of the river.

The faded 13c charter from St Pauls

The first recorded mention of Wapping occurs in the records of St Paul's Cathedral in the early years of the thirteenth century. A charter dated between 1218 and 1226 records the surrender of Wapping Mill by Terricus of Aldgate to the Dean and Chapter. The name appears in Latin as *Wapping'*, with the apostrophe signifying a shortened ending. The whole name was probably Wappinges, which appears elsewhere, a derivative of the Saxon Waeppingas.

It seems that by this time the marsh had been reclaimed by the building of an earthwork wall. In 1324 it was stated that:

> *"a certain person of antient time Lord of the Mannour of Stebenhethe... did by his industry recover a certain Marsh there, containing about an hundred Acres of Land."*

The Lord of the Manor was the Bishop of London. It is not clear what the people of 1324 regarded as ancient time; but it could hardly have been less than 100 years, and indeed, the tide-mills would not have functioned had the land not been embanked.

There is no record of exactly where Wapping Mill stood but it became a landmark along the river and was probably at Wapping Ness, where the Thames Police boatyard now stands.

Terracus rented the mill from the Dean and Chapter, apparently in return for the monopoly of grinding corn for the common bakehouse at St Paul's. He appears to have had difficulty in making it profitable as he fell behind with the rent and had to surrender the monopoly in 1231 in return for a reduced rent. About ten years later he was given permission to make a grant of the mill to the Hospital of the Knights of St Thomas of Acon.

The Knights were a crusader order with a house in Cheapside on the site of the birthplace of St Thomas Becket, to whom the house was dedicated and whose sister, Agnes, had made over the site to the order. They also had a house in the crusader stronghold of Acon in the Holy Land, which gave them their name.

The Hospital came to hold a good deal of property in Wapping until the dissolution of the monasteries.

The Dean and Chapter of St Paul's Cathedral held property in the area, with a house in Shadwell with its own chapel. They also had a tide-mill of their own at Ratcliffe.

St Paul's and the Knights of St Thomas of Acon probably both ground corn for their own use in their tide-mills.

To the west there was another tide-mill, with two wheels, at the bottom of Nightingale Lane. Known as the Crash Mills, in 1233 it was the subject of a dispute between the Priory of the Holy Trinity Aldgate and the Rector of St Dunstan's Stepney, Nightingale Lane being the border between them. The dispute was resolved when they agreed to share the tithes.

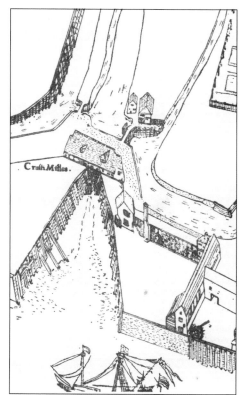

Drawing of Crash Mills at Wapping

21

Another tide-mill, by the Iron Gate of the Tower, was part of Queen Matilda's grant to St Katharine's Hospital but when the moat was built around the Tower, the brethren lost their mill.

Stow recorded that, after Richard I had left to fight in the third crusade in 1189, his regent, the Bishop of Ely, William Longchamp, strengthened the defences of the Tower and:

> *"caused a deepe ditch to be cast about the same, thinking...to have environed it with the River of Thames. . .and the Mill was removed that belonged to the poore brethren of the Hospitall of Saint Katherine.. .which was no small losse and discomnoditie."*

The Hospital later acquired another tide-mill, however.

There were at least some advantages in having the Tower as a neighbour. Henry III moved the royal menagerie, which Henry I had started at the Manor of Woodstock, to the Tower.

The menagerie was open to the public and must have provided a great deal of novelty for the people of the surrounding area. According to Stow, the menagerie consisted of *"Lions and others"*.

In 1251 a polar bear was brought from Norway and was allowed to swim in the river and catch fish. Then, in 1255, the King of France sent a *"great present"* of an elephant. People flocked to see the elephant, which was claimed to be the first ever seen in England.

King of France's gift elephant

There was some inequality in the provision made for food in the Tower. According to Stow, Edward II provided *" that prisoners in the Tower should have for their food, twopence a day for a knight and a penny for a squire"*. The polar bear received fourpence and the lions and leopards sixpence.

22

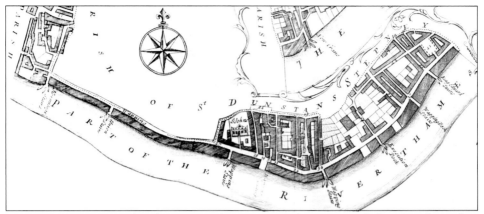

Earliest known map documenting "The Hermitage" (from Stow's London)

Being a low lying marshy area, Wapping was always liable to be flooded. The first recorded flood was on the night of 31st December 1323 when there was a *"mighty floud, proceeding from the tempestuousness of the Sea, which overflowed all the Banks."*

An inquisition into the causes of the flood was held at St Katharine's in 1324, at which evidence was given about the reclamation of the marsh in the previous century. There was an earthwork wall with *"Banks, Ditches Sewers Etc."* Each landholder was responsible for maintaining his section of the wall and there were wallreeves to see that the work was done.

By this time the feudal system was breaking down as land was granted freehold, that is without services, and evidence showed that families from the City of London were holding land in Wapping.

Of the 100 acres reclaimed, 42 acres had been granted freehold by charter, of which 32 acres were held between John Gisors, John Peyrun and Maude de Canterbury, half an acre by Walter Crepyn and 10 acres by the Hospital of St Thomas of Acon.

The Gisors family was prominent in the City. Sir John Gisors was twice mayor and Constable of the Tower and the de Canterbury and Creypn families both provided Aldermen to the City.

The remaining part of the reclaimed land was farmed by villeins from the Manor of Stepney. The freeholders blamed them for the flood, claiming that, while they had kept their own part of the wall in good repair, the villeins had been negligent in maintaining theirs, which had allowed the breach to occur in the wall. The freeholders therefore claimed that the Bishop of London should be responsible for the cost of repair.

It was not stated which part each held but evidence was given that the breach had been made by the outgoing tide. It would therefore seem that the freeholders held the east side and the villeins the west side of Wapping. The west side was more liable to flooding, being lower lying and open to the combined forces of the tide and the flow of the river.

The inquisition found in favour of the freeholders but a subsequent case in the Court of King's Bench decided that each landholder should be responsible for repairing his own section of the wall.

Similar problems recurred later as it proved beyond mediaeval skill to keep the water out of the western part of the marsh, which became known as Wapping-in-the-Wose. There was more success on the eastern side where there was a hamlet on Wapping Wall.

Local history group inspecting Black Death grave

In 1348 the Black Death reached London and then spread across the country killing between a third and a half of the population.

There was not enough room in the churchyards to bury all the dead and Nicholas, the Prior

24

of the Holy Trinity, Aldgate, made available a plot of ground in East Smithfield for the burial of the dead of the area. This churchyard was on what later became the site of the Royal Mint, which was then in the Tower.

A chapel was built and Edward III founded the Abbey of St Mary Graces on the site. The Abbey was run by Cistercian monks and was sometimes known as Eastminster, intended to match Westminster. Eastminster survived as a road name until 1988 when it disappeared in the new Tower Hill traffic scheme.

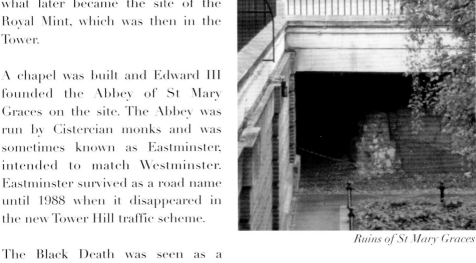

Ruins of St Mary Graces

The Black Death was seen as a punishment from God and led to a tightening of discipline, which had become lax in many religious houses. The Cistercians wore white habits and aimed to live in strict poverty.

The area was a favoured one for religious houses. A convent had been set up nearby in 1293 by the Nuns of the Order of St Clair, known as the *"poor Clares"* or minoresses, who gave their name to the Minories.

There were also several hermits in the area, who lived a life of prayer and poverty in small cells or chapels which they passed from one to the other. In Wapping, there was a hermit named John Ingram who lived at the bottom of Nightingale

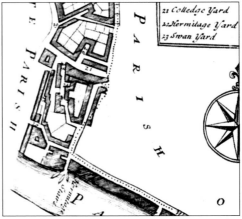

Detail of Stow's map of London with "Swan" and "Hermitage" references

Queen Philippa pleads for the Burghers of Calais with Edward III

Lane from 1371 to 1380 in a hermitage called the Swan's Nest. This area of Wapping became known as the Hermitage.

Hermits usually established their cells near a religious house, so that, if they did not receive enough alms to live on, the monks or nuns would take care of them.

The Wapping Hermitage was conveniently near to St Katharine's, which had also undergone some tightening of discipline under the patronage of Edward III's wife, Queen Philippa.

Queen Philippa's Ordinances laid down that the monks and nuns of St Katharine's were to take vows of poverty, chastity and obedience and wear the habit of religion bearing the emblem of

St Katharine. They were to wear black or dark colours and no brother was allowed to converse alone with a sister. The remaining occupants of the Hermitage were scholars and bedeswomen. The latter were to wear grey and were not allowed to go out alone or to stay out at night.

Stricter rules were laid down about the use of funds and a scheme of rebuilding was undertaken. A new church was built with carved wooden stalls in its chancel. These stalls were to see several changes of location.

Stalls in the Church at St Katharine's today

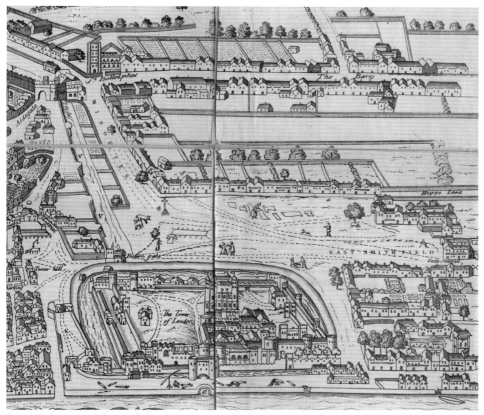

Ralph Aggas's map of 1560

By the reign of Queen Elizabeth I the whole of Wapping's waterfront had been built up as a result of Vanderdelft's drainage scheme.

John Stow, who lived in Aldgate, wrote the first description of Wapping, beginning at St Katharine's, which he described as:

John Stow

> *"S. Katherine by the Tower of London, an Hospitall with a Maister, Brethren, and sisters and Almes women, founded by Matilde, wife to King Stephen, not suppressed but in force as afore...being now of late yeres inclosed about, or pestered with small tenements, and homely cottages, having inhabitants, English and strangers, more in number then in some citie in England."*

He went on:

*"from this precinct of S. Katheren to Wapping in the Woze, and
Wapping it seife, the usual 1 place of execution for hanging of
Pirats & sea Rovers, at the low water marke there to remaine, till
three tides had overflowed them, was never a house standing
within these 40 yeares: but since the gallowes being after remooved
farther off, a continuall streete, or filthy straight passage, with
Alleyes of small tenements or cottages builded, inhabited by saylors
victualers, along by the river of Thames, almost to Radcliff, a good
mile from the Tower."*

The gallows was removed to Execution Dock, but the practice of
allowing three tides to come over the bodies seems to have been
discontinued. The executed pirates were buried at St Botolph's
Aldgate, whose records show that one, Thomas Edwards, was
hanged and buried on the same day.

Stow also described:

*"Nightingall lane (which runneth south to the Hermitage, a
Brewhouse so called of a Hermite sometime living there.)"*

He defined both Wapping and Shadwell as being:

"on the south side of the high way to Radcliff."

St Katharine's was still having trouble with its Masters. Elizabeth
appointed another layman, Dr Thomas Wilson; but he closed St
Katharine's choir school, sold the right to hold the Fair to the
City of London, and was preparing to sell other rights when the
inhabitants of the Precinct drew up a *"Petition of the inhabitaunts
against Dr Willson"*, which they sent to the Queen's chief secretary.
Sir William Cecil:

*" we your pore orators the inhabitaunts of the precincte of Saynte
Katheryns nygh the Tower of London, that for asmuche as doctor
Willson, now mr. of the hospitall of Saynt Katheryns intendeth as
muche as in hym lyeth for a pryvate gayne of a sume of money to
hym to be paide for ev'more to sell and put awaye to the lorde*

mayor of the citie of London, and his bretheren and the comynaltie therof, all the whole liberties, rights, franchiesies, royalties and pryveleges belonginge to the saide howse or hospitall which doth apperteyne, and is p'cell of the dowry of the quenes of this reaime, which thing not onely wil be a greate losse and hurte to the prerogative of the succession of the quenes of this reaime, but also of the utter subversion and extinguishinge of the true foundation therof, and to the utter impoveryshinge decay and undoing of us your saide orators and oure posteryties here after to come."

As a result of this *"spirited petition"* Wilson's plans were stopped and Elizabeth later appointed Dr Julius Caesar as Master. He proved a much better Master and provided a carved pulpit at his own expence.

Dr Julius Caesar's pulpit

With the monasteries gone, parishes became responsible for their own poor relief and St Katharine's Hospital was made responsible for poor relief in the Precinct.

By then the rest of Wapping was divided between St Dunstan's Stepney and St Mary's Whitechapel, which had originally been set up as a chapel of ease to St Dunstan's, so that people would not have so far to go to church; but it had become a parish church and taken over the western part of Wapping, which became known as Wapping Whitechapel, while the eastern part, which remained in St Dunstan's parish, was known as Wapping Stepney.

Wapping was still liable to flooding at high tides, which led the queen to encourage development along the river, although in general the government tried to prevent the spread of London beyond its walls. Those who built houses along the Wapping waterfront were responsible for keeping the river wall in good repair.

The houses were built of wood, and there was a new danger of fire among all the combustible materials stored in the warehouses along the river.

With the threat of invasion by the Spanish Armada, the men of Wapping had the duty of providing a watch for the Tower and if necessary defending it. The Lieutenant of the Tower was responsible for mustering the men of Tower Hamlets for the militia in time of emergency.

The men of Wapping were however more likely to serve at sea. Elizabethan Wapping had taken on a strong maritime character, with seamen of all ranks living there. The historian Richard Hakluyt consulted sea captains in Wapping about naval matters.

There were galleons in the river and a thriving trade, as from being an isolated marsh on the edge of the Manor of Stepney, Wapping became the most populated and prosperous part of the area, and Elizabethan explorers set sail from Shadwell.

Overseas trade could no longer be legally carried on in Wapping, however, as an Act of Parliament of 1558 restricted imports and exports to legal quays west of the Tower; but there was always inland trade, and smuggling.

Monument to Elizabethan explorers in Shadwell Park

Claes Jan Visscher panorama attributed to Thomas Wyck

The development described by Stow can be seen in the early seventeeth century panorama attributed to Thomas Wyck, which shows a glimpse of the Wapping riverfront beyond the Tower.

The increase in population led to a demand from the people of Wapping Whitechapel for a church of their own. In 1615 they petitioned the Bishop of London for permission to build a chapel of ease, stressing the distance to the parish church, which they said led to:

> *"the frequenting Ale-Houses on Sundays by the looser sort of People."*

They also mentioned:

> *"the Danger of Fire or Floods which may happen in their Absence while at Church."*

Permission was given and a chapel was built dedicated to St John the Evangelist. It was consecrated by the Bishop on 7th July 1617.

The chapel cost £1,600, which was raised partly by local people and partly by collections outside. The historian John Strype mentioned:

> *"the Citizens of London, being worthy Benefactors toward it."*

He also recorded that there was:

> *"A fair Gallery built on the South side of the Chappel, with Part of the Benevolence that was given for the Use of the Chapel by the Mariners that went to the East Indies, Anno 1616 in the Royal James."*

Charles I

The first minister was Richard Sedgwick. The Rector of Whitechapel, Richard Gardiner, had a window put in at his own expense; but the people soon agitated for their chapel to become a parish church, arguing that they were already providing for their own poor.

On 24th July 1629 Wapping received an unexpected royal visit when Charles I was out hunting. Strype recorded:

> *"King Charles having hunted a Stagg or Hart from Wansted in Essex, killed him in Nightingale Lane, in the Hamlet of Wappin, in a Garden belonging to one - who had some Damage among his Herbs, by Reason the Multitude of People there assembled suddenly."*

Wapping retained its maritime character. One resident was Admiral William Rainsborough, born in 1587, who was one of the elder brethren, then the Master, of Trinity House, while it was in Ratcliffe.

Admiral Rainsborough led a large fleet to the Mediterranean in 1637 to deal with slave traders. Slavery was not a one-way traffic. Barbary pirates, or corsairs, from North Africa raided European ports to take Christians and sell them as slaves in the Ottoman Empire. They even raided ports in the English West Country, especially Cornwall, as well as attacking British merchant ships and fishing vessels. Captives could be redeemed by paying a ransom of about £45, which was several times the price of a slave. This was far more than an ordinary family could afford and funds were raised for the ransoms of slaves but this only made the trade more lucrative. Rainsborough and his fleet blockaded the Barbary port and rescued 350 English men, women and children held by the corsairs. He died in 1642 and was buried in St John's Churchyard.

Rainsborough's fleet was financed by ship money, a tax which was one of the grievances that led to the outbreak of civil war in 1642. As part of London's defences against the king, Wapping had "*A Bulwark & half on the Hill at the North end of Gravel Lane*". *Gravel Lane* was later called *Old Gravel Lane* to distingush it from *New Gravel Lane* further east. (In 1939 the names were changed to *Wapping Lane* and *Garnet Street*.) Wapping was strongly Protestant in the seventeenth century and supported the puritan parliamentarians.

Thomas Rainsborough, the Admiral's son, who was born in Wapping, started his career in the navy, but transferred to the army, which was not unusual at that time. He became a colonel in Parliament's New Model Army and took part in the debates on the future shape of the country which followed the army's defeat of the royalists.

Eastern part of London's defences

Colonel Rainsborough sympathised with the Levellers, who advocated reforms, most of which did not come about for over two hundred years, such as giving all men the right to vote in parliamentary elections.

Thomas Rainsborough

In a famous speech on 29th October 1647, Rainsborough said:

> *"For really I think that the poorest he in England hath a life to live as the greatest he; therefore truly sir, I think it is clear that every man that is to live under a government ought first by his own consent put himself under that government."*

Rainsborough's ideas were too advanced for his fellow roundheads. In 1648 he was killed by a band of royalists but suspicions have arisen that there was collusion between them and the parliamentary forces. Thomas Rainsborough's body was brought to Wapping for burial, accompanied by a large crowd. Afterwards there was anti-royalist rioting for two days.

The next year King Charles was beheaded and puritan, republican government was firmly established. This brought danger to St Katharine's. Both its royal connections and its monastic past were repugnant to the puritans and there were demands for its suppression:

> *"It ought at all events to be suppressed, monkery being the root of all iniquity."*

St Katharine's survived, but with a puritan preacher, Richard Kentish.

St John of Wapping

William Morgan's panorama

In 1660 Charles II was restored and during his reign William Morgan drew up a map of London that extended to the east to show the whole of Wapping. Morgan's map has a panorama depicting the Wapping riverfront and a street plan showing how the area had developed.

Along the river was Wapping Street, Stow's *"filthy straight passage"* ("straight", spelt *"strait"* in later reprints, meant long and narrow), and leading down to it, Nightingale Lane, Old Gravel Lane, and New Gravel Lane. There were developments along the river and on the sides of the streets but most of the drained marsh between them remained *"Pasture Grounds."*

Samuel Pepys recorded several visits to Wapping in his diary, the first in 1661 to attend the funeral of Captain Robert Blake. Pepys recorded visiting Sir William Warren's timberyard and in 1666 did business with Sir William over buying lighters for the Fleet. He usually travelled by boat along the river.

Samuel Pepys

Wapping had by then become a residential area for City businessmen, but it had a mixed population, including ordinary seamen, who rioted in 1667 because they had not been paid.

In 1665 the great plague ravaged London. In his *"A Journal of the Plague Year"*, which was written in 1722, but from contemporary sources, Daniel Defoe recorded that Wapping at first appeared to have escaped the plague, and that:

> *"Some people fancied the smell of the pitch and tar, and such other things as oil and rosin and brimstone, which is so much used by all trades relating to shipping, would preserve them."*

The Journal shows the close contacts between Wapping and the City as Defoe went on to record that the people in Wapping:

> *"received their friends and relations from the city into their houses."*

As a result the plague came to Wapping in September and October and raged violently there.

Defoe said the people took to the river:

> *"As the richer sort got into ships, so the lower rank got into hoys, smacks, lighters and fishing boats."*

He related a story that three men set out from the Hermitage to escape the plague and obtained a certificate that they had not been in London, which he remarked,

> *"though false in the common acceptance of London in the country, yet was literally true."*

This shows that by then Wapping was commonly regarded as part of London, although it was not part of the City.

The Great Fire of London viewed from Wapping

Many of the plague victims were buried in the churchyards of St John of Wapping and St Paul's Shadwell, where a chapel had been established about 1656.

The next year saw the great fire of London; but on this occasion

Wapping escaped, as the fire was stopped at the moat of the Tower, a fortunate circumstance for Wapping as the White Tower was full of gunpowder. The people of Wapping were able to watch in safety the old St Paul's Cathedral burning in the midst of the City; but they had several *"dreadfull Fires"* of their own soon after, as most of the houses were built of timber.

St Paul's, Shadwell became a parish church in 1670, its parish including Wapping Wall. The people of Wapping Whitechapel continued to agitate for St John's to become a parish church. They claimed that they could not afford to pay tithes to St Mary's and maintain their own church as the inhabitants were *"chiefly Seamen and depending on Sea Trade"* which had been affected by recent wars.

St Paul's, Shadwell

The rector of Whitechapel opposed the proposal, replying that the inhabitants of Wapping *"are accounted a Wealthy People"*. The inhabitants denied this and retorted that *"the Rector doth wholly neglect the Pastoral Care."*

They achieved their aim in 1694 when the old chapel of St John became the parish church for what had previously been Wapping Whitechapel; but the central part of Wapping remained in the parish of St Dunstan's Stepney.

St John's church was inside the churchyard and slowly sinking into the marshy ground.

St Katharine's was still having trouble with its masters. It was claimed that Sir James Butler was misappropriating the funds and allowing the church to fall into ruins. Queen Catherine, the wife of Charles II, sent the Lord Chancellor to look into the complaints. As a result Sir James was removed, new rules drawn up and a programme of rebuilding undertaken.

Piety & Piracy

St Katharine's school was revived and in 1695 St John's set up a charity school in Cock Alley, near the church. It was rebuilt in 1760.

Wapping remained strongly Protestant and bands were raised there to support those in the City who were trying to force the king to agree to the exclusion of his brother, the Duke of York, who was a Roman Catholic, from the sucession. The attempt failed however and the Duke later became James II.

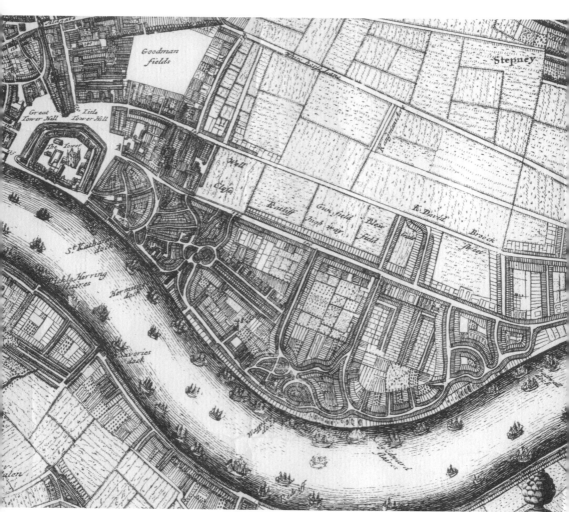

Wapping in the William Morgan Map

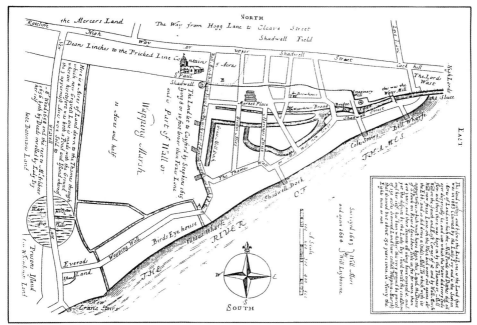

Map showing part of disputed land in Shadwell

The uncertainties about the distribution of the shares in the land reclaimed in Vanderdelft's drainage scheme, added to some later uncertainty as to precisely what area it had covered, led to a good deal of litigation in the seventeeth century.

Lady Ivy, who was *"famous for Wit, Beauty, and Cunning in Law"*, brought several law suits claiming parts of Wapping and Shadwell.

She was born Theodosia Stepkins and her father, a City businessman, lived in Wapping. She claimed that her ancestor, Thomas Stepkins, had been one of the original owners of the land, and that they had agreed with Richard Hill that he should have 53 acres as the share he had inherited from Vanderdelft. She further claimed that Hill had later made over the land to Stepkins.

In one action she claimed land between Old Gravel Lane and New Gravel Lane and in another, land at Prusom's Island, but in her most famous case she claimed the land to the east of Foxes Lane, which ran down from St Paul's Church to Wapping Wall.

Most of this land is now the King Edward VII Memorial Park; but in the seventeeth century it was held by the Dean and Chapter of St Paul's Cathedral.

St Paul's Shadwell had been built to the north with the help of Thomas Neale, who was Master of the Mint, then still in the Tower of London.

Shadwell water works

Neale had leased part of the disputed land and on it built the Shadwell Water Works, which supplied piped water from the river to houses from the Tower to Stepney, by means of a pump driven by four horses.

This made the site very valuable, and Lady Ivy won a suit in which she claimed to have inherited it from Stepkins.

Neale, however, brought a suit in which he claimed that her case had been based on forged documents. This *"Famous Tryal"* was heard in the Court of King's Bench in 1684 before the Lord Chief Justice, Sir George Jeffreys.

Jeffreys did not at that stage have the reputation of being a hanging judge. Although a large crowd gathered outside Westminster Hall, there does not appear to have been any hostility towards him.

Several local people appeared as witnesses to describe the area and gave evidence that the cellars were often flooded at exceptionally high tides. One witness, Kemp, described Shadwell as it had been in his youth, 50 years earlier:

"Several places of it were gardens and orchards; some places had houses, chiefly to the northward, some good houses and orchards. "

The witnesses did not show any particular fear of the judge, who conducted the case with exemplary fairness. It was shown that one of Lady Ivy's documents was a forgery and she lost the case. She was later tried for forgery but acquitted as she convinced the jury that she had produced the document in good faith.

After Charles II died he was succeeded by his brother, James II. This led to a rebellion in the West Country and it was when Jeffreys was sent to try the rebels that he acquired his reputation as a hanging judge. About 250 rebels were hanged.

Jeffreys became Lord Chancellor but in 1688 James II was replaced by his daughter Mary and her husband, William of Orange, in the Glorious Revolution. Jeffreys disguised himself as a sailor and attempted to escape abroad.

He was, however, recognised in Wapping and apprehended. There are several different versions of his capture - one says he was recognised in the *Red Cow* in Anchor and Hope Alley, which was where Reardon Path is now.

Jeffreys was hated in strongly Protestant Wapping, not so much for his conduct in the West Country but because he was suspected of having helped James in an attempt to return the country to Roman Catholicism. Jeffreys steadfastly denied this charge.

He had in fact refused to become a Roman Catholic himself, although his refusal reportedly led James to cancel plans to make him Earl of Flint. In his will Jeffreys stressed that he had lived and died a member of the Church of England.

Jeffreys was already terminally ill with a stone in the kidneys and he died in the Tower in April 1689.

Judge Sir George Jeffreys

Detail of Wapping in John Rocque's map of London

When John Rocque drew his map of London in 1746, Georgian Wapping had taken shape. By then improved methods of building foundations had allowed new houses to be built in brick.

The fields between the main roads were still open and the map shows them planted with trees but there were further developments along the riverfront and along the roads leading into Wapping including new roads such as Broad Street (now Reardon Street), a new wider road leading out of the older and narrower Anchor and Hope Alley. Broad Street became a favourite place for naval officers to live, and leave their families while they were at sea, as there was a Navy Pay Office there.

St Katharine's had been restored but the restoration did not please everybody. One critic concluded:

"we might hold up the interior of the late new east window...for still greater reprehension, as being in a state of comparison with the original sublime objects around it. "

On the north side of the Ratcliffe Highway, a new church, built by Nicholas Hawksmoor, was consecrated in 1729. This was St George-in-the-East whose parish comprised most of the old Wapping Stepney.

It was a parishioner of St George's, Henry Raine, a wealthy brewer, who in 1719 founded Raine's Charity Schools in Charles Street (now Raine Street). The schools catered for 50 boys and 50 girls and there was a hostel, called Raine's Hospital, where some of the girls boarded.

Raine's School

Raine introduced a scheme whereby each year, two girls, chosen by lot, received a dowry of £100 each when they married. Raine recorded:

> *"the fortunate maid that got it burst into tears from excess of Joy."*

Considering how much £100 was worth, this was hardly surprising. It would have bought a house in Wapping then.

In 1725 John Newton was born in Wapping. He spent his boyhood there before going to sea. He became the captain of a slave ship but later saw the error of his ways and became one of the leaders of the anti-slavery movement. He was ordained into the Church of England and wrote the words of the hymn Amazing Grace:

> *"Amazing grace (how sweet the sound) That saved a wretch like me! I once was lost, but now am found, Was blind but now I see."*

Slaves were bought from tribal chiefs in West Africa and most were taken to the West Indies to be sold. A few were brought to England as personal servants or even sold here, usually in riverside inns, until 1772 when a test case clarified the law and stopped the practice.

A slave named James Somerset, who had been bought in Virginia, was brought to England by his owner. He ran away but was recaptured and was being held in irons in a ship on the river, to be taken back to America.

The Abolitionists applied for a writ of Habeas Corpus and the judge, Lord Mansfield, ruled that there was no such status as slavery under English law and that the man was free when he set foot in England.

William Cowper wrote:

> *"Slaves cannot breathe in England, if their lungs Receive our air, that moment they are free; they touch our country, and their shackles fall."*

Slavery went on in the colonies, which had their own laws, until 1837.

Wapping had a mixed population, with a good many negro seamen to whom the rector of St George's, Dr Herbert Mayo, paid special attention. One of his curates said:

> *"I suppose no clergyman in England ever baptised so many black men and mulatoes...The attachment of these poor people to him was very great."*

Wapping's strongly Protestant past was continued in a Dissenting Chapel in Nightingale Lane and there was a strong Quaker presence with a Meeting House in Brewhouse Lane.

Hannah Lightfoot

One of the Quakers was Matthew Lightfoot, whose daughter Hannah was supposed to have been secretly married to George III in 1759, before he became king. The story is however very unlikely as one of the few things that can be definitely ascertained about Hannah is that she was married in 1753 to a young man named Isaac Axford. This marriage is recorded in the records of St George's Chapel, Hyde Park Corner, London.

Axford was still alive in 1759, so that if Hannah went through a marriage ceremony with George it was bigamous. The whole story is highly improbable and more likely one of the pieces of scandal that the period delighted in.

There were 36 public houses along the Wapping waterfront, including the *Ramsgate Trader* at Wapping Old Stairs.

Wapping Old Stairs was a place of embarkation for sailors and famous for the shanty:

> *"Your Molly have never been false, she declares,*
> *Since last time we parted at Wapping Old Stairs."*

In one tavern lived Hannah Snell, who was famous for having disguised herself as a man and joined first the army and then the marines.

Several public houses showed their links with the Whitby coal trade in names such as the *Coal Cat* and, at a later date, the *Prospect of Whitby*.

Pirates were still hanged at Execution Dock, including Captain Kidd, who was hanged there in 1701.

At Execution Dock was a public house called the *Bell*, which was the birthplace of Elizabeth Batts, who was baptised in St John of Wapping in 1741.

The Whitby coal trade brought to Wapping a young seaman named James Cook, who was apprenticed to John Walker, a Quaker shipowner. Cook probably met Elizabeth when she was a child and, according to a story told by the painter Constable, he promised to marry her when she grew up.

He did marry her in 1762 and they lived in Shadwell during the early years of their marriage. Their eldest son, James, was baptised in St Paul's Shadwell. They moved to Mile End in 1765.

James Cook joined the Royal Navy in Wapping in 1755 and went on to a career of exploration and finally to his death in Hawaii in 1779.

Elizabeth lived until 1835.

Captain James Cook

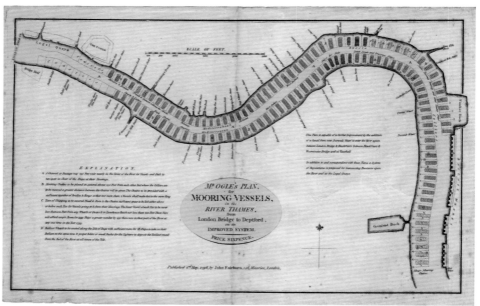

Mr Ogle's plan for improved mooring

In 1783 Dr Samuel Johnson advised James Boswell to explore Wapping. Dr Johnson knew the area well and was a friend of Dr Henry Mayo, the minister of the Dissenting Chapel in Nightingale Lane.

In 1760 St John's Church was rebuilt outside its churchyard as the old chapel had sunk so far into the ground that, as J. P. Malcolm recorded:

> *"Thomas Goodland, parishioner, had a seat at one end of the church, so situated that graves in the burial-ground were higher than his head."*

Malcolm was generally uncomplimentary about Wapping, saying:

> *"The best streets in it are so narrow, so wet, so badly paved, so despicably parsimonious, that the passenger hardly dare lift his eyes to the intermixed mansions of the rich ship-bakers, mast-makers, boat-builders block-makers, mathematical instrument makers, and Wapping landlords and ladies, lest he should honour them with unintentional prostration."*

At the time when St John's was rebuilt, the rector was Dr Francis Willis, who had become rector in 1748. Unlike most clergymen, who were Doctors of Divinity, Willis was a Doctor of Medicine. He was interested in mental illness and became "mad doctor", a sort of early psychiatrist, to George III during the king's first bout of insanity.

St John of Wapping

It is recorded that the king greeted him at their first meeting by saying:

> *"You have quitted a profession I have always loved, and you have embraced one I most heartily detest. "*

Willis replied:

> *"Our Saviour went about healing the sick. "*

"Yes, " said the king:

> *"but he had not £700 a year for it. "*

Willis believed in a *"mild system"* of treatment but this involved putting the king in a strait-waistcoat or tying him into an iron *"Chair of Correction"* that he ironically called his Coronation Chair.

Dr Francis Willis

As Willis explained:

> *"when my gracious sovereign became violent, I felt it my duty to subject him to the same system of restraint as I should have adopted with one of his gardeners at Kew. "*

The King recovered and Willis was disappointed to receive only a pension of £1,000 per annum, when he had been expecting £1,500 and a baronetcy.

During the King's later bouts of insanity, he was attended by Willis' son, John.

Willis remained nominally rector of Wapping until 1800 but he never took a wedding at St John's and the ministry was carried on by two curates.

Shadwell enjoyed a period as a health resort. The spring which fed the well, believed to be St Chad's Well, was claimed to have healing properties and a spa was established by Cutthroat Lane where people went to take the waters.

The Royal Menagerie

The Royal Menagerie was still in the Tower, though by the end of the century it cost a shilling to see the animals, which included a lion and lioness called Marcus and Phyllis, and their cub, Nero, who was very tame and a great favourite.

During the eighteenth century an Irish population grew up, mostly in Cable Street, north of the Highway and in 1768 there was a riot by Irish coal-heavers that led to a man being unintentionally killed. As a result, several of the rioters were hanged.

The Irish were the victims during the Gordon Riots of 1780. These riots, led by Lord George Gordon, were anti-Catholic and raised the cry of *"no Popery."* In an orgy of drunken rioting, Newgate Prison was burned down and the prisoners were released, not only from Newgate but from the Fleet, Marshalsea and King's Bench prisons. Rumours were spread that the lunatics had been released from Bedlam and the lions from the Tower. The Irish had a chapel in Virginia Street which was burned down by the rioters, an incident mentioned by Dickens in *Barnaby Rudge.*

St Katharine's also attracted the attention of the rioters *"having been built in Popish times"* and preparations were made to burn it down but this scheme was thwarted by the London Association and the ringleaders were hanged on Tower Hill.

A greater danger was facing the old hospital. By the end of the century the restriction of imports and exports to the legal quays was hampering trade and plans for wet docks in the area were already being discussed.

The restrictions had led to so many ships being tied up in the river, waiting to load or unload their cargoes, that it was claimed it was possible to walk across the river on their decks. This led to a great deal of pilfering.

John Herriot, a local JP, persuaded some West India merchants to put up the money for a police force to deal with the pilfering, and in 1798 the Marine Police was set up in Wapping, the first regular police force in the world.

Their rowing galleys, with constables and a surveyor, kept watch on the river, as their successors in the Marine Support Unit of the Metropolitan Police still do today.

Wapping Police Station in 1798

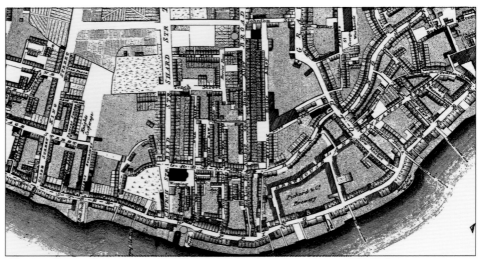

Horwood's map featuring ⬤ Gun Dock and ⬤ No. 4 Broad Street, Bligh's home

In 1785 William Bligh came to live in Wapping with his wife, Elizabeth, and their daughters, four-year-old Harriet and one-year-old Mary. Bligh had sailed with Captain Cook in the *Resolution*, on his last, tragic voyage but was currently on half pay from the Royal Navy and commanding merchant ships owned by his wife's uncle.

Captain William Bligh

The Bligh family moved into No. 4 Broad Street. Horwood's map of 1799 shows the house numbers and No. 4 was on the west side just south of Johnson Street, now Chandler Street. The land tax records for Lower St George's show that Bligh was paying £18 per annum in rent and £1.13s in land tax. He lived next door to Elijah Goff, a City business man, who was paying the same amount in rent and tax.

Most other householders in the vicinity were paying less, the average rent being about £10 and land tax 10s 4d. The likelihood is, therefore, that Bligh and Goff lived in houses that were larger than those round them.

Bligh was no doubt told the story of the capture of Judge Jeffreys in nearby Anchor and Hope Alley. Being a west countryman he probably approved.

Broad Street was in the parish of St George-in-the-East and in 1786 Mrs Bligh had another daughter, Elizabeth, who was baptised in St George's on 5th May.

Bligh commanded a West Indiaman, the *Britannia*, and had with him Fletcher Christian, who visited him in Broad Street while they were ashore and played with his children.

A plan was then being drawn up to transplant the breadfruit which Captain Cook had described, from Tahiti to the West Indies. It was hoped breadfruit would be better able to withstand hurricanes than the native plantain.

Sir Joseph Banks, who had sailed with Cook on his first voyage, was one of the promoters of the scheme and in May 1787 he visited Wapping to look at a ship named the *Bethia*, which was moored off Wapping Old Stairs. With him were Mitchell, the Assistant Surveyor of the Navy Board, and David Nelson, a botanist who had sailed with Cook and Bligh in the *Resolution*.

Breadfruit growing at the Eden Project, Cornwall

The *Bethia* was a ship of 216 tons. They decided that she would be suitable for the purpose and she was purchased by the Navy and renamed His Majesty's Armed Vessel *Bounty*.

Bligh was appointed to command the *Bounty* and took Christian as a master's mate, a senior midshipman. He also took with him a young midshipman, Peter Heywood, who was going to sea for the first time. Heywood stayed with the Bligh family before the *Bounty* sailed and sent his washing to a Mrs Duncan in the Hermitage.

Bligh took as his gunner William Peckover, who lived nearby in No. 13 Gun Alley. He had sailed with Cook on all three of his voyages of discovery. David Nelson was appointed botanist for the voyage.

HMAV Bounty

When Bligh sailed in the *Bounty* in December 1787, he left his wife and children in Wapping. Mrs Bligh was pregnant when he left and in 1788 she had twin girls, Frances and Jane, who were baptised in St George's on 6th June.

After the *Bounty* left Tahiti, Christian led the famous mutiny in April 1789 when Bligh and those loyal to him were cast adrift in an open boat.

Peckover said he was wakened from his sleep by a *"confused noise"* and met David Nelson, who told him *"the ship was taken from us."* Peckover thought they had been attacked by natives but Nelson said *"It is by our own people, Christian at their head"*. When Peckover was asked what he intended to do he replied *"to get home if I could"*. He realised that those who stayed in the ship would *"all be deemed pirates"*. He and David Nelson both went with Bligh in the open boat. Heywood remained in the ship, as he said *"to be starved to death, or drowned, appeared inevitable if I went in the boat."*

Bligh, Peckover and Nelson all reached Timor safely after a voyage of four thousand miles in the *Bounty's* launch but Nelson died of a fever in the East Indies. Bligh wrote:

"The Mango Trees are now in blossom and some of the Jambolang, and the Bushes in general indicate the advance of Spring. All these circumstances recall to me the loss of Mr Nelson and the object of my Voyage, which at times almost bear me down."

Bligh and Peckover returned safely to Wapping.

In May 1790 the first dramatic representation of the mutiny, *The Pirates*, was put on at the Royalty Theatre in Well Street, on the north side of Ratcliffe Highway. Bligh was played by the actor-manager, Ralph Wewitzer, and Christian by William Bourke, who appeared as a hornpipe dancer in another part of the programme. *The Pirates* included an *Otaheitean Dance* by the chorus.

The Royalty was famous for special effects and showed the *Bounty* sailing down the Thames. The theatre later staged *The Death of Captain Cook* and *He Died for his Country or Nelson Victorious*, which depicted the Battle of Trafalgar and the death of Nelson.

Royalty Theatre interior

Soon after his return, Bligh and his family moved to Lambeth but his contact with the area continued. In 1791 he was given a second chance and recruited men for his new ship, *HMS Providence*, in the *Roundhouse*, a public house in New Gravel Lane. One of the surgeon's mates, Robert Ridgway, came from Shadwell.

The voyage was successful. The breadfruit was safely delivered to the West Indies and is still grown there. It is now imported into England and sold in Deptford Market.

While Bligh was away on his second breadfruit voyage, Peter Heywood, having been found in Tahiti, was brought back to England to face a court martial. Heywood wrote to Mrs Bligh protesting his innocence and asking her to retrieve his washing from Mrs Duncan. He was found guilty but recommended to mercy and pardoned.

Christian sailed with eight of his followers and some Polynesians to Pitcairn Island where they formed a settlement but quarrels led to all but two of the men dying violent deaths. When the settlement was discovered in 1808, there was only one mutineer left, John Adams, who took the opportunity to write to his brother, Jonathan, a waterman who lived in Upper Gun Alley, Wapping and worked at Union Stairs, Wapping.

It is not known why Bligh moved from Wapping, but it was probably because plans were already being discussed for the building of wet docks in the area, which would lead to the demolition of the house where he lived

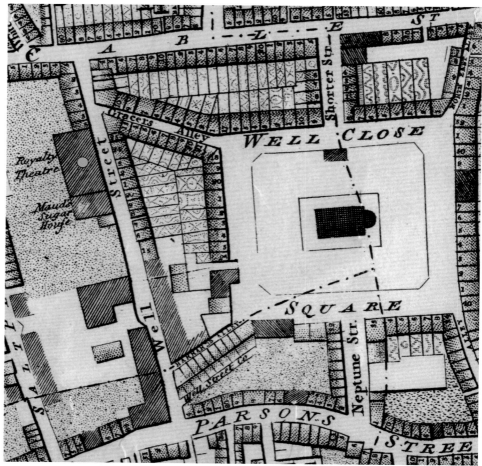

Horwood's map showing ● Royalty Theatre in Well Street

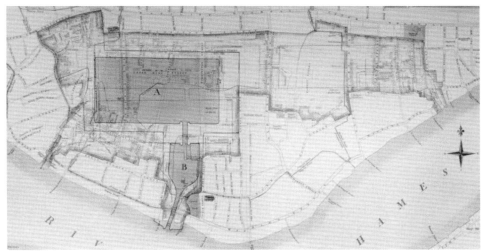

Plan for London Docks based on Horwood's map

In 1800 the London Dock Act was passed authorising the building of a wet dock in Wapping.

In the previous year an Act had been passed allowing the building of docks on the Isle of Dogs but that was still a sparsely populated area. Wapping had a large population and many of them were displaced by the new dock.

The first London Dock was built between Old Gravel Lane and Nightingale Lane with an entrance at the Pier Head, near Wapping Old Stairs, and another at the Hermitage Basin, on the site where the Crash Mills had stood.

A reprint of Horwood's map with the plans for the London Dock superimposed upon it shows how it took up a large part of the central area of Wapping. While the wet dock itself was largely in space that was previously drainage fields, it was surrounded by quays, warehouses and offices which spread into the surrounding area where many houses were demolished, including those on the west side of Broad Street where Bligh had lived. Part of St John's Churchyard was also taken for the dock, necessitating a reburial of the dead.

The London Dock Company was given powers of compulsory purchase and used them to purchase land from Raine's Schools which resulted in the schools being improverished and the dowries being discontinued. The schools moved out of Wapping to Cannon Street Road, then later to Arbour Square, then Bethnal Green.

The Shadwell Water Works, whose horse-drawn pumps had been replaced by a steam engine in 1774, was also purchased and demolished.

The London Dock Company was granted a monopoly of tobacco, wine, brandy and rice. Tobacco and liquor were subject to excise duty and had to be kept in bonded warehouses with strict security. This led to the building of massive walls around the docks.

The London Dock was designed by Daniel Alexander, the architect of Dartmoor Prison. The dock tended to look like a

prison from the outside but the houses built for dock staff on the Pier Head were and still are a fine example of Regency architecture. Underground were the wine vaults with architecture like the crypt of a Gothic cathedral. Tasting was allowed and it became fashionable to go down to the vaults and sample the wine.

A wine tasting at London Docks

The riverfront remained in the hands of other companies, still operating from wharfs and tidal docks, such as Wapping Dock, which was never part of the London Docks.

The last hangings at Execution Dock were on 17th December 1830 when two men were hanged for mutiny and murder on the high seas. The name disappeared a few years later.

The first ship sailed into the London Dock on 31st January 1805. Two years later, the Grand Surrey Basin was opened on the south side of the river, and the need was felt for a river crossing nearer than London Bridge. In 1824 an Act of Parliament was passed authorising the building of a tunnel under the Thames. This scheme was completed in 1843, the work of Marc Isambard Brunel and his son, Isambard Kingdom Brunel. The original plan for a

Thames Tunnel under construction

tunnel which traffic could use was never implemented, as the approach roads were not built but the tunnel was used as a foot tunnel until later in the century.

The painter Joseph Mallord William Turner owned a public house in Wapping, the *Ship and Bladebone* in New Gravel Lane. He often visited the area and in 1839 took the opportunity to board a river steamer and paint the *Fighting Temeraire* as she was towed down to Rotherhithe to be broken up.

Turner's famous painting shows the old wooden warship, that had fought at Trafalgar, being towed by a steam tug, the smoke from the tug's funnel filling the sky against a setting sun. It was symbolic of the old and the new.

Joseph Mallord William Turner

Plan for docks on site of St Katharine's

The building of the London Dock led to a proposal from the St Katharine's Dock Company to demolish the old church and hospital and everything in the Precinct to build a wet dock there.

The scheme led to a public outcry as people were:

"...horrified at the proposal to destroy the ancient Hospital and Church and to render a large population homeless."

A pamphlet argued:

"on every principle of propriety and decency the preoccupancy of the soil by St Katharine's church for seven centuries...ought to direct the steps of the dock Company elsewhere."

The Bill which put forward the scheme provided for compensation to be paid to freeholders and leaseholders, but most of the people in the Precinct were only tenants and no provision was made for giving them any assistance in finding new homes. This was likely to be more difficult as the building of the London Dock had led to overcrowding in the surrounding area.

The people of the Precinct drew up a petition to Parliament:

"The Persons whose names are hereinbefore set forth, are only actuated by a desire to convince the Honourable Members of the House of Commons of the irremediable ruin to which the passing of the Bill hereinbefore alluded will entail upon themselves and Families, many of whom rest their future prospects in life upon the connexions which themselves and Ancestors have formed in the neighbourhood, and which, will be wholly destroyed , in the event of Docks being constructed in the Precinct of Saint Katharine's..."

"There is another circumstance which is a subject of deep regret to the Inhabitants, viz. the destruction of their Ancient Church, and the disturbing the remains of their Ancestors and Families, a circumstance which cannot but distress every person possessed of the least feel ing...Every circumstance pleads against the destruction of the Ancient Collegiate Church and Precinct. The fact of New Churches being necessary in consequence of the increased population - of its being attached to a religious foundation which has for more than 700 years been adorned and protected by a series of Royal Patronesses - its being one of the few Memorials of the piety of our Ancestors which have escaped the great Fire of 1666 - Its being an object of considerable interest for its Architecture and the various Relics of early Art it contains..."

"The Inhabitants (whose names are hereinbefore set forth) in conclusion leave their Case to the wisdom and justice of the Honourable Members, trusting that the Legislature will never allow an humble but deserving Class of People to be reduced to penury and want, and their feelings ouraged by any measure which is not called for by Public necessity."

The petitioners added their own reasons, such as:

"My ancestors and relatives have resided in the precinct 140 years."

"I am 80 years of age, and the Docks will turn me out of a comfortable home."

"7 fatherless children entirely destitute."

"The Docks will wholly destroy our connexion whereby we are making a good living."

Three proprietresses of Dame schools pleaded that they would lose their livelihood, so including St Katharine's own school, there must have been at least four schools in the Precinct.

The first Bill was withdrawn and there was great rejoicing:

"On Tuesday Evening, June 1, 1824, the Precinct of St Katharine presented a scene of great gaiety, originating from the rejoicings of the inhabitants at the withdrawing of the Bill. The houses of every street, lane and alley were illuminated."

The Bill was, however, re-introduced in the next session and the old hospital was betrayed from within.

The building of the London Dock had made the area less attractive as a residence and the St Katharine's Dock Company offered the Master, Sir Herbert Taylor, and members of the Chapter, funds for premises in Regent's Park, with greatly increased stipends. The Chapter accepted the offer.

St Katharine's demolition

The hospital was without a queen as its patroness. George IV hated his wife, Queen Caroline, and would not let her take on the patronage but took it on himself after her death. He gave his consent.

The Act was passed and the last service was held in the old church on Sunday 30th October 1825. The Gentleman's Magazine recorded:

"After the concluding Amen, the whole congregation pressed forward through the arch which once sustained the roof-loft, to the chancel, and that portion of the building soon exhibited a moveable mass of people, filling up every corner: the former sacredness of the now desecrated edifice did not prevent the expression of just feelings of indignation against the ruthless destroyers of the ill-fated building, and more particularly when the majestic organ, to be broken up on the morrow, pealed forth the anthem God save the King."

In a month nothing was left of the old church and over 2,000 people were turned out of their homes.

Construction of St Katharine's Dock

St Katharine's Dock opened in 1828 but it was, like the London Dock, built for sailing ships. When Thomas Hosmer Shepherd had published his *Views of London* in 1827, his drawing of the Tower of London had shown a paddle steamer going past.

The opening of St Katharine's Dock

In 1830 William IV became King. He had been a naval officer and was said to have "a Wapping air".

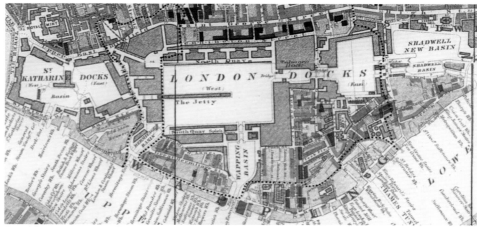

Booth's poverty map of London covering Wapping

During the nineteenth century additional docks were built in Wapping. The original dock became known as the Western dock when another, known as the Eastern dock, was built between Old Gravel Lane and New Gravel Lane in 1828. The Old Shadwell Basin was built in 1831, and the wider New Shadwell Basin in 1858, to admit larger ships.

The London Docks made Wapping an island. It could only be reached by crossing one of four bridges: at Pier Head, Old Gravel Lane, New Gravel Lane and Wapping Wall.

Riverfront warehouses

High walls closed in the docks, hiding them from view, so that for those who did not work in them, a glimpse of the inside could only be caught from the bridges. There the tall clippers could be seen, whose masts stood up above the walls.

Huge warehouses were built along the riverfront, cutting off the River Thames from the people of Wapping so that it could be seen only from a few remaining public houses such as the *Town of Ramsgate* and the *Prospect of Whitby*. The warehouses made Wapping High Street dark, all along to the bridge by St

Katharine's Dock. From there could be seen the buildings designed by Thomas Telford, with their great iron columns, and the water that covered the site of the old church and the Precinct. The dock soon proved inadequate and the Ivory House was added, with additional quays, in 1860. High warehouses continued, on both sides of St Katharine's Way, to the

Telford's warehouses at St Katharine's

Iron Gate of the Tower. By then the moat had been drained.

The lions and other animals had followed St Katharine's move to Regent's Park, leaving only the ravens at the Tower but there was something to be seen in a waxwork display showing the kings of England. The mint had been removed to Tower Hill.

The docks brought about a change of population, as labourers from all over the country and from Ireland, came, first to build the docks and then, to work in them. The Irish population increased so that they made up a third of the total by the middle of the century.

Nineteenth century Wapping was not so uniformly poor as has sometimes been assumed, as Booth's map shows. There was a private school, *Frederick Roessler's Academy*, in Bird Street (now Tench Street) in the middle of the century.

Wapping also retained its artistic connections, with Whistler living there while he was painting his Thames Set.

Nevertheless, with a large proportion of the population relying upon casual labour in the docks, there was bound to be a great deal of poverty, especially when trade was bad or adverse weather prevented ships from coming up the river into the docks.

Wapping by James McNeill Whistler

69

Mayhew reported:

"It is a sight to sadden the most callous, to see thousands of men struggling for only one day's hire, the scuffle being made the fiercer by the knowledge that hundreds out of the number there assembled must be left to idle the day out in want."

Charles Dickens

For those who could not feed themselves and their families, the Poor Law provided the workhouses condemned by Charles Dickens. St John's and St George's provided one each.

Dickens made several visits to Wapping. He collected wine from St Katharine's Dock and was taken on the river by the Thames Police in a four-oared rowing galley. In *The Uncommercial Traveller* he described a visit to St John's workhouse in a chapter entitled *Wapping Workhouse*. He wrote:

"Long before I reached Wapping, I gave myself up as having lost my way, and, abandoning myself to the narrow streets... found myself on a swing-bridge looking down at some dark locks in some dirty water...with a scum that was like the soapy rinsing of sooty chimneys."

Dickens said that among the pauperesses:

"I regretted to identify a reduced member of my honourable friend Mrs Gamp's family."

He found that in the sick-rooms:

"the attendance was kind and patient" and *"The wretched rooms were as clean and sweet as it is possible for such rooms to be."*

On his way out of Wapping he went to St George's workhouse and:

"found it to be an establishment highly creditable to those parts."

In a chapter entitled *A Small Star in the East*, he described a visit
to the East London Children's Hospital, then in Ratcliffe:

> *"I found the children's hospital established in an old sail-loft or
> storehouse, of the roughest nature, and on the simplest means...but I
> saw the sufferings both of infancy and childhood tenderly assuaged."*

In another chapter, Dickens described an emigrant ship in the
Shadwell Basin, taking emigrants to Mormon Salt Lake City in
the USA.

In general he was not very complimentary about the district:

> *"Down by the Docks, they 'board seamen' at the eating-houses, the
> public-houses, the slop-shops, the coffee-shops, the tally shops, all kinds
> of shops mentionable and unmentionable - board them, as it were, in the
> piratical sense, making them bleed terribly; and giving no quarter."*

He was also uncomplimentary about the high church services at
St George-in-the-East, which had provoked riots, describing them
as *"fancy-dressing and pantomine-posturing"* but those who
indulged in this *"miserable trifling"* were to bring relief to the area.

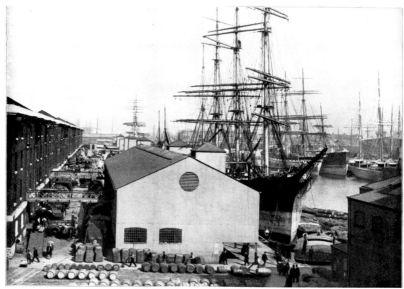

The London Docks c1890

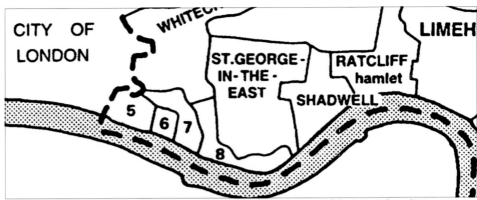

Parish Map 1819 showing: 5 Tower, 6 St Katharine's, 7 St Botolph's, 8 St John of Wapping

The docks brought new problems to Wapping. In earlier days seamen had either homes and families to go to, like Cook and Bligh, or they remained aboard ships moored in the river.

After the docks were built large numbers of seamen were turned off their ships into the surrounding area. As they had usually been paid off and had plenty of money, there soon grew up a criminal class to plunder them, as Dickens had noticed.

It was said at the time:

"A full volume would not suffice to exhibit the records of debauchery and crime with which the history of but one street in the East of London is associated. That street is the Ratcliffe Highway."

Ratcliffe Highway about 1890

Criminals preyed on the seamen who arrived with full pay packets and there was *"drunkeness and prostitution, robbery and violence, ignorance and unbelief."*

In 1856 the rector of St George-in-the-East set up a mission to counter these problems. The missioner was the Rev. Charles Fuge Lowder. He had intended to join a foreign mission but was persuaded to undertake a home mission instead. A mission house was set up in Wellclose Square, where an Anglican order, the Sisters of the Holy Cross, was established; but the mission came to concentrate on the part of Wapping which lay in St George's parish. A chapel was built in Calvert Street (now Watts Street) and dedicated to the Good Shepherd; but was known as the *"Iron Chapel"*. The mission staff strove against threats of violence from the criminal elements, and from extreme Protestants, who objected to the ritual in the chapel.

The congregation increased until the Iron Chapel, which held 200 people, was too small for them and the new church of St Peter's London Docks was built. St Peter's was consecrated in 1866. Its parish consisted of all the parts of Wapping which did not lay in the parish of St John.

Interior of St Peter's London Docks

Soon after St Peter's was consecrated there was a terrible outbreak of cholera, due to the contamination of the water supply. The clergy and sisters worked ceaselessly among the sick, without regard for their own safety. Fortunately none of them caught the infection. Charles Lowder frequently carried sick children in his arms to St George's Hospital, the old workhouse infirmary. He was called *"the Father"* and from that time the clergy at St Peter's took that title.

Father Lowder looked bitterly at St Katharine's in Regent's Park, pointing out that it had been set up for:

> *"the poor of the East of London, especially of our own neighbourhood And yet it is actually permitted that such a body should rest at ease in Regent's Park with scarce an attempt to benefit anyone but themselves, while the East of London is calling out."*

Queen Victoria did appoint a clergyman, the Rev. J. Blunt, as Master but the hospital remained, *"a kind of aristocratic Almshouse."*

After the cholera epidemic, St Peter's congregation continued to grow. Father Lowder stayed there for the rest of his life, though his health was undermined by the hard work and bad conditions. He died while on holiday in Zell-am-See, Austria on 9th September 1880.

Father Wainright
(Harry Darby, author's father on right)

In 1884 the Rev. Lincoln Stanhope Wainright became vicar. He had been a curate at St Peter's since 1873 and said he wished only to follow in Fr Lowder's footsteps, *"though a very long distance behind."*

For the next 45 years Fr Wainright devoted himself completely to his parishioners. He never took a holiday or, if he could help it, remained out of the parish overnight. He gave away all his money and possessions to the poor, even his coats and shirts and the coal from his scuttle.

The thing that everyone noticed about Fr Wainright was that *"he was always so happy."* He always said that Wapping was the most lovely place in the world and that he never wanted to be anywhere else.

The people of Irish descent living in Wapping were mostly Roman Catholics and were not neglected. Fr Matthew came to preach temperance, as excessive drinking was a great problem at the time. By 1879 they had their own church, St Patrick's, in Green Bank and their numbers increased rapidly with continued immigration from Ireland. There were nuns attached to St Patrick's so that the habits of religion were once more seen in Wapping. Both churches used outdoor processions as part of their ministry and proclaimed their faith through the streets of Wapping. People became accustomed to seeing banners and statues being carried through the streets.

St John's School continued and St Peter's and St Patrick's both established schools, continuing the work of the churches in the education of the area.

In 1902 the American author, Jack London, was in London to report on the Coronation of King Edward VII. He stayed, disguised as a sailor, and later wrote *The People of the Abyss*, in which he said:

> *"No more dreary spectacle can be found on this earth than the whole of the 'awful east', with its Whitchapel, Hoxton, Spitalfields, Bethnal Green, and Wapping to the East India Docks... Here lives a population as dull and unimaginative as its long grey miles of dingy brick. Religion has virtually passed it by, and a gross and stupid materialism reigns, fatal alike to the things of the spirit and the finer instincts of life."*

He could not have spent much time in Wapping, nor visited the churches, or he would have found them full and ministering to the spiritual and material needs of the people.

St Peter's London Docks

St Patrick's Wapping

Opening of Tower Bridge 30th June 1894

By the beginning of the twentieth century, steam ships had replaced the sailing ships for which the Georgian docks had been built. The London Docks had been adapted for steam with new quays and most ships entered by the New Shadwell Basin, so that they did not have to negotiate the bend in the river round Wapping. St Katharine's Dock was less suitable for adaptation to steam and came to be used largely for warehousing cargoes brought up river by barge.

Local horse and lorry traffic

Goods were taken to and from the docks and the riverside warehouses by horse-drawn waggons which rumbled through the streets of Wapping with their heavy loads.

By then Tower Bridge had been built, providing a crossing for traffic as well as pedestrians and Brunel's tunnel was used by steam trains in the early days of London's underground. The line was electrified in 1913.

The outbreak of the First World War in 1914 was the harbinger of change. At first, trade increased in the docks but the attacks by

German U-boats on shipping in the Atlantic led to ships being diverted to ports in France and there was slackness in the London Docks.

Jack London wrote of *"The People of the Abyss"*:

> *"It is absurd to think for an instant that they can compete with the workers of the New World. Brutalized, degraded, and dull, the Ghetto folk will be unable to render efficient service to England... Neither as worker nor as soldiers can they come up to the mark when England, in her need, calls upon them."*

They were about to prove him wrong.

Many young men from Wapping joined up and many were killed. Three who joined the King's Royal Rifles on the same day in 1914 were all killed the next year.

Air raids became a danger and on 2nd June 1915 the German airship, *Graf Zeppelin*, was seen bursting into flames in the sky. Later there were air raids by German planes aimed at the docks, which made Wapping a target of attack. When the maroons sounded, people mostly went down to their basements. No bombs fell on Wapping itself but one fell nearby in Royal Mint Street, near the Tower of London. A great deal of noise was also made by the Tower Gun, a large anti-aircraft gun on Tower Wharf.

Anti-aircraft gun 1914-1918

With the return of peace, the London Docks returned to normal and trade increased.

Much of this trade was with ports in northern Germany, especially Hamburg, and German ships were seen in the docks once more.

London Docks Eastern Dock

During this period the docks were at their busiest and from the bridges steam ships could be seen, loading or unloading their cargoes. Cargoes from all over the world came to the London Docks. The vaults were still full of barrels of wine and wool from Australia was laid out on the skin floor of Tobacco Dock, though it was brought up from the Royal Docks by barge or by road.

Tobacco Dock

When a ship entered the docks, or went from one dock to the other, there was a *'bridger'*. The bridge was raised and all traffic came to a halt while people waited for the ship to go through. This was usually done fairly quickly but if barges were going through there was a lengthy wait as they were pushed through by long poles.

Much of the traffic was still horse-drawn but lorries were appearing. They loaded by the wharfs in Wapping High Street or entered by the huge wooden gates of the docks to take goods in and out.

Flooded moat of Tower of London 1928

Wapping was still liable to flooding. In 1928 there was a tidal wave which refilled the moat of the Tower of London and flooded all the basements in the area. In 1929 Fr Wainright died and Wapping was flooded with tears.

With the thirties came the depression. There was sometimes idleness in the docks and unemployment among the people.

By that time people of Irish extraction made up two-thirds of the population of Wapping, the highest proportion it was to reach.

The churches continued their work until better times returned and the docks were busy again.

A beach was made in front of the Tower Wharf, where children could play on the sand at low tide. There was a large rowing boat that provided trips through Tower Bridge, a short way down the river and back. For longer voyages, the Eagle Steamers left from Tower Pier for Southend and Margate.

Persecution in Europe had led to successive waves of Jewish immigration into the East End. This was increased by the persecution in Nazi Germany. Jews did not work in the docks and consequently did not settle in Wapping but large numbers settled in Shadwell and the areas to the north, many opening shops there. The presence of this different culture on the other side of the bridges added to Wapping's insularity.

The appearance of Wapping was changed by the building of council flats and most of the road names were changed, so that historic names like Nightingale Lane, Old Gravel Lane and New Gravel Lane disappeared.

Tower Beach 1930s

First day of the Blitz 7th September 1940

In September 1939, Wapping was once more at war.

The vicar of St Peter's London Docks, the Rev. A.H. Luetchford, wrote in the parish magazine:

"everywhere there is evidence of a splendid calm among the people."

Children were evacuated from London just before the outbreak of war. The children from St Peter's went to Brighton, Sussex. Fr Luetchford wrote:

"From all accounts they thoroughly enjoyed the experience."

For a time nothing much seemed to happen and children began to drift back home as there were no raids on London.

9th September 1940 was the 60th anniversary of the death of Fr Lowder and plans were made to commemorate the event but as Fr Luetchford remarked:

"Our plans for September were somewhat upset by the air attack on London."

On Saturday 7th September, a party of friends from St Peter's went on a pilgrimage to Fr Lowder's grave in Chislehurst, Kent. From Chislehurst Common they saw the great daylight raid on the docks, in which incendiary bombs were dropped. They returned to find the docks on fire and the bridges closed. They were unable to get back into the parish and had to take refuge in the crypt of St George-in-the-East. The German bombers returned that night, guided by the fires, to drop high explosive bombs. The party returned on Sunday morning to find St Peter's Church damaged by blast. When they arrived:

> *"a number of women and girls were sweeping up the Church in a most matter-of-fact manner and none could have imagined the ordeal they had just been through."*

There were more raids in the days that followed. The bridges and the underground were closed so that the only way to get in or out of Wapping was by river. Some people were evacuated by boat from the Tunnel Pier to Kew.

The gas and electricity supplies were cut off and water from the hoses of the firemen poured down the streets, mixed with liquor from the docks, where the casks had burst with the heat.

A contributor to St Peter's parish magazine wrote:

> *"That first week was unpleasant. For two or three days it was very hard to get in or out of the Parish; we had no water, gas, electricity, and very few shops...The 'hub of our universe' is the Feeding Centre in the Senior School. It was almost, if not quite the first, to open in London, and still continues under the management of Miss Lloyd Holland assisted by some of the teachers from St Patrick's Schools, and a number of devoted and untiring voluntary helpers."*

The bombing continued night after night for the rest of the year. Fr Luetchford and his staff went from shelter to shelter, regardless of the danger, in the worst of the raids, bringing comfort to the people.

St Peter's church suffered heavy damage when a bomb fell on the Mission House next to it. One of the Sisters of Charity working

Firefighting in St Katharine's Dock c1940

there, Sister Catherine Elizabeth, was killed.

The danger of flooding prevented the people of Wapping from using the underground station but they took cover in the huge wharfs. Fr Luetchford described them:

"On the whole they seem as safe as anything can be: they are reasonably dry, not too overcrowded, and mostly inhabited by families known to each other. The larger ones have had some entertainment, dances, pictures and Christmas parties for the children."

The shelterers in the Hermitage Wharf were concerned that some people, who did not bother to go to the shelter when there was a raid, turned up when entertainment was laid on. They recorded in their Minutes:

"A suggestion was made that tickets should be issued to regular users of the Shelter in order to prevent the gate-crashing of individuals who had already made a convenience of the Shelter for dancing & entertainment."

There was a midnight mass in the Orient Wharf on Christmas Day and St Peter's Parish magazine recorded:

"The quiet and devotion of the people was remarkable and the singing of the Christmas hymns most moving."

Heinkel-111 above Wapping

The people of the Hermitage Shelter had their Christmas party on 28th December. On 29th December there was a great raid on the City of London and that night the people of Wapping once more saw the City in flames. The Hermitage, being on the edge of the City, was heavily bombed and the Hermitage Wharf was hit by high explosive and incendiary bombs. The river wall was breached and the water poured in but the people were evacuated safely.

They complained:

> *"The people are now dispersed among St John's Shelter, Colonial & Orient. Many Hermitage people would like to be reunited in some convenient alternative Shelter."*

During the raids, St John's church received a direct hit. It was not rebuilt and the parish was united with St Peter's. St George-in-the-East was badly damaged in a raid in 1941.

By then the raids were less concentrated on the docks, though one of the heaviest raids on London was in May 1941, just before Hitler turned his attack on Russia. After that there were occasional raids, mostly on moonlit nights, until near the end of the war when the V1 and V2 rockets were launched against London. One of these hit the Hermitage and several people were killed. Peace finally returned in May 1945.

Bomb damage to St John of Wapping

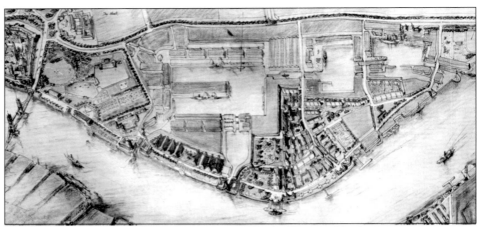

Ling's artistic impression of Wapping as proposed in the Abercrombie plan

In 1943, while the war was still on, the County of London Plan was drawn up for the reconstruction of bomb-damaged London. This plan became known as the *'Abercrombie Plan'* after one of its authors, Professor Patrick Abercrombie.

Abercrombie   In relation to Wapping, the Plan proposed:

> *"...that the river front of Stepney, from the Tower to King Edward VII Park, should in the main be freed for open space and riverside amenity. The future of the Katharine's Dock has, we understand, been under consideration for some time. If it were decided that the dock is redundant, we suggest that it might become the site of a riverside open space for Stepney as well as a park-setting for the Tower of London... There would also be sufficient areas to provide walks and attractive rest gardens.*
> *"Ultimately, on the east, a green strip would supplant the narrow stretches of warehouses...and bring the redeveloped areas of Wapping into association with the river. The new open space would link up the existing parks and provide a continuous treed riverside walk from the Tower to King Edward VII Park. The removal of the warehouse 'wall' separating the residential area from the river would transform this district."*

The Abercrombie Plan met with the approval of the people of Wapping but its imaginative war-time proposals were never implemented.

After the war there was a new wave of immigration as people arrived from the West Indies. This was not so strange to Wapping as to other parts, because Wapping had a long history of being a home for black people. The newcomers settled in with little trouble. They were followed by other immigrants, mostly from Bangladesh, who also settled in peaceably. The schools accommodated the children from the new communities and St Peter's outdoor procession was made more colourful by the presence of children whose families came from many parts of the Commonwealth of Nations.

St Peter's Day procession, Wapping Lane

The Abercrombie Plan had anticipated that St Katharine's Dock would close, but at that time it had been expected that the London Docks would continue. The London Docks grew busy again after the war and Wapping seemed to be entering a new period of prosperity. The Dock Labour Scheme gave dockers a security of employment they had never previously enjoyed and they were among the best-paid manual workers.

London Docks in the 1960s

One of the problems of this period was that the council flats had been built without garages, as no one had thought that the tenants would have cars. The streets of Wapping soon became full of parked cars.

With the movement of trade further down river and the introduction of containers for cargo, however, it became clear that the London Docks were likely to close as well as St Katharine's Dock. By 1969 both the London and St Katharine's Docks had closed. Some of the dockers went to Tilbury to work, some took

85

redundancy payments but many moved out of Wapping, as their way of life had come to an end there.

For years the old docks stood empty. The original Pier Head entrance to the London Docks was filled in but the docks remained, sad and derelict, with no ships on the water. St Katharine's Dock was similarly empty, with its great black columns and the water that still covered the site of the old church and hospital which had been sacrificed for the dock.

London Docks in the 1980s

London Docks in the 1980s

St Katharine's new home at Ratcliffe, new chapel interior with ancient furniture

While the days of St Katharine's Dock were coming to an end, the institution it had replaced returned to its old area.

St Katharine's Hospital had been dissolved before the First World War and replaced by the Royal College of St Katharine while Queen Alexandra was patron. The chapel remained at Regent's Park but the college was provided with premises at Bromley Hall in Brunswick Road, Poplar, where it undertook the training of nurses in infant and child welfare. The change was intended to restore St Katharine's to the East End but in fact the new premises were as far from the original site as Regent's Park. Nevertheless, the college did useful work in a deprived community in Poplar.

This work continued during the Second World War. Poplar, like Wapping, was a target in the attack on the docks and Bromley Hall was damaged during the Blitz of 1940.

After the war, and with the introduction of the National Health Service, it was decided that the college was no longer needed in its current form. It was again reconstituted, under the patronage of Queen Mary, as the Royal Foundation of St Katharine.

The chapel in Regent's Park became the Danish Church in London and the Foundation's work and worship were reunited. At the same time, the opportunity was taken to bring the Foundation nearer its original site. St James Church, Ratcliffe had

St Katharine's Chapel in 2010

been bombed and was not to be rebuilt but its vicarage, a converted Georgian manor house, survived. The old manor house provided the basis for new premises for the Royal Foundation of St Katharine, with the former school hall serving as a chapel until a new chapel could be built.

Fr St John Groser, who had served most of his ministry in East London, became Master. He renewed St Katharine's traditional care of the elderly by pioneering post-war welfare work among the old people of Stepney and starting a *"meals on wheels"* service - taking food to the old people of the area. A programme of retreats and conferences was also established, reviving St Katharine's educational work.

When St Katharine's Dock closed, a suggestion was made that the Royal Foundation might return to its original site, but this proved too expensive and the Foundation remained in Ratcliffe, about one mile from the original site.

Queen Mother in 1952

By 1952 a new chapel had been built. It was designed in a plain modern style, but the fourteenth century carved wooden stalls and the Elizabethan pulpit, which had been taken to Regent's Park, were brought back again and installed in the new chapel.

After Queen Mary's death in 1953, Queen Elizabeth the Queen Mother became patron and under her patronage another tradition was revived when St Katharine's was placed in the care of a religious order. The Foundation was entrusted to the care of the Community of the Resurrection, an Anglican order. The Community was joined by sisters of the Deaconess

Community of St Andrew so that, for a time, St Katharine's was once more staffed by men and women religious, with its worship and work of service to the community reunited.

The Deaconess Community of St Andrew was later replaced by the Sisters of the Church and the Community of the Resurrection decided to withdraw at the end of 1992; but St Katharine's continues, as it has for the last eight hundred years.

St James Vicarage, now part of St Katharine's, in 2010

Wapping Wood, formerly the Eastern Dock of London Docks

St Katharine's Dock was eventually redeveloped as a marina in the 1970s. The water was retained and used mostly by large, luxury cruisers. The Victorian Ivory House was converted to provide shops and restaurants. Nothing remained of Telford's Georgian buildings except the Dockmaster's house. They were replaced by office blocks. Some of the original columns were used to build a chapel but this was later turned into a café.

Tower Hamlets Council purchased the London Docks in 1969 and built houses on the quays around the Eastern dock. The water was drained out of the dock and grass and trees planted, restoring the site to what it had been in the eighteenth century.

On the river, sail returned in the form of yachts as the Thames was used for pleasure-boating and became the scene of leisure, rather than work, while the Thames Police continued to patrol the river in their motor launches.

The first warehouse conversion along the riverfront was Oliver's Wharf, an interesting building in Victorian Gothic style. It was converted into flats by a young architect, Anthony Goddard. Later

St John's and the Gun Wharf were also converted into flats.

St George-in-the-East church was imaginatively rebuilt in a style suited to the new situation but retaining its traditional appearance. A smaller church was built inside the Hawksmoor walls.

In 1980 planning was transferred to the London Docklands Development Corporation (LDDC) and private housing was built on the Western dock. A canal was built through the area where the water had flowed, to recreate something of the former atmosphere.

Oliver's Wharf flats

A shopping village was built in Tobacco Dock, which had been part of the original London Docks. Shops and restaurants were provided in converted buildings near where sheepskins had once been laid out and, at the lower level, the old wine vaults were converted to more shops and restaurants. The prices charged were, however, so high that the shops had to close, leaving the place almost empty.

The water was retained in the Shadwell Basin and used for boating activities by local groups but the housing around the Basin, on the quays, was a private development.

Further private development took place along the riverfront, where the Abercrombie Plan was abandoned Flats were built that looked like wharfs, recreating the Victorian riverfront. There was little access to the river, so that it remained cut off from the area.

The new private flats and houses were expensive and brought back City workers to the area, so that Wapping's community was once more a diverse one.

St George-in-the-East

Police in Wapping during the printer's strike

On the south side of The Highway, News International's new premises were built, which became known as *"Fortress Wapping"* during the bitter print worker's strike there in the 1980s.

It was intended that the population in the Wapping area should increase from about 3,500 to over 10,000 but the recession of the 1990s put something of a damper on these plans. The building of more offices was then approved by the LDDC. The building of one block led to the destruction of the remains of Shadwell's Roman watch tower, on the grounds that not enough of it remained to be listed. A new school was built in the Hermitage and St Peter's School was provided with new premises.

At the end of the decade there was another grab for Wapping and houses were built on every available piece of land. St John's School was converted to town houses and the Church to luxury flats, both too expensive for local people although both had originally been built through public subscription, much of it raised locally.

Hermitage Site, redeveloped with war memorial

The beginning of the new millennium in 2000 saw the last piece of riverfront, where the Abercrombie concept might have been implemented, handed over to developers. This was the historic Hermitage riverside, between Pier Head and Hermitage Bridge. The LDDC sold the land to developer Berkeley Homes. Tower

Hamlets Council approved their plans to build high rise blocks on the riverside, cutting out the view of the river and Tower Bridge from the people in the social housing opposite. A small piece of land next to Hermitage Basin was spared for an open space, with a memorial to the civilians killed by the bombing. This was, ironically, in the shape of a dove of peace; Hitler's aim in launching the Blitz had been to force Britain to make peace.

With the death of the Queen Mother in 2002, Queen Elizabeth II became patron of the Royal Foundation of St Katharine, which provided for conferences and retreats. The churches continued their work, bringing the old and new communities together and working for harmony among the different sorts and conditions of people, so that there was still piety in Wapping. There was no lack of piracy, though of a different sort, as Wapping's fate was, as always, shaped by its proximity to the City of London.

St Katharine's Dock Marina

93

BIBLIOGRAPHY

ANGLO-SAXON CHRONICLE *In Two of the Saxon Chronicles* (Ed J. Earle)

BARTON, Nicholas .*The Lost Rivers of London*, 1962.

BEDE, The Venerable. *Ecclesiastical History of the English People.*

BOSWELL, James. *Life of Johnson.*

BROODBANK, Sir Joseph G. *History of the Port of London*, 1921.

BURNEY, Fanny. *Journals and Letters.*

CHARLTON, John (Ed). *The Tower of London: Its Buildings and Institutions.*

DARBY, Madge, Waeppa's People, 1988. Judge Jeffreys and the Ivy Case, 1989. Captain Bligh in Wapping, 1990. Hermitage Shelter Minutes (Ed) 1990. The Royal Foundation of St Katherine

COMMONS JOURNAL *V.498.XI.52* (Establishment of St John of Wapping)

DEFOE, Daniel. *A Journal of the Plague Year*, 1722

DICKENS, Charles. *The Uncommercial Traveller.*

DUCAREL, Andrew. *History of the Royal Hospital and Collegiate Church of St Katharine.* 1784.

DUGDALE, Sir William. *The History of Imbanking and Drayning of Divers Fenns and Marshes.*

ENGLISH PLACE NAME SOCIETY, *Place Names of Middlesex.*

FALK, Bernard. *Turner the Painter: His Hidden Life*, 1939.

FIELD, John. *Place Names of Greater London*, 1980.

FITZSTEPHEN, Walter. *Descriptio Nobilissimae Civitatis Londoniae.* (Printed as an Appendix to Stow's Survey. Translated in the Everyman Edition)

FORBES, Thomas Rogers (Ed). *Chronicles from Aldgate.* (St Botolph's parish registers 1558-1625)

GIBBS,M.(Ed) *Early Charters of St Paul's Cathedral.*

GILDAS. *The Works of Gildas. Translated in Six Old English Chronicles.* Ed J.A.Giles.

GROOM, Frederick and Tear. Lesley (Ed) *Raine's Retrospect 1719 - 1969.*

HAKLUYT, Richard. *Principal Navigations.*

HILL, G.W. and Frere W.H. (ed) *Memorials of Stepney (St Dunstan's Vestry Minutes 1579 - 1662)*

HOWELL, T. *State Trials X* (Including Lady Ivy's Trial for the Greater Part of Shadwell, 1684)

JAMISON, Catherine. *History of the Hospital of St Katharine by the Tower of London*, 1952.

JONES, Lincoln S. Colonel Thomas Rainsborough, 1992.

KERRIGAN, Colm. *History of Tower Hamlets.*

KINGSFORD, C.L. (Ed) Chronicles of London.

LAND TAX RECORDS, Guildhall, London.

LOPTIE, W.J. A *History of London*, 1883.

LONDON & MIDDLESEX ARCHAEOLOGICAL SOCIETY Transactions Vol V: Coote, H.C. *The English Guild of Knights and their Socn.* P477. Birch, G.H.*Stray Notes on the Church and Parish of St Mary Matfelon.* P514.

LORDS JOURNAL, *VI,580,644,VIII,684,IX,81.* (Establishment of St John of Wapping)

MACALPINE. I and Hunter, R. *George III and the Mad Business*, 1969.

McDONNELL, Kevin. *Mediaeval London Suburbs*, 1978.

MAITLAND, William. *The History of London*, 1756.

MALCOLM, J.P. *Londinium Redivivum*, Vol IV,1802.

MAYHEW, Henry. *London Labour and the London Poor*, 1851.

MENZIES, Lucy, *Father Wainright*, 1947.

NEWCOURT, Richard. *An Ecclesiastical Parochial History of the Diocese of London*, 1708.

NICHOLS, John. *Account of the Royal Hospital and Collegiate Church of St Katharine near the Tower of London*, c1808.

OXFORD DICTIONARY OF ENGLISH PLACE NAMES. *4th Edition* 1959.

PARIS, Matthew. *Chronica Majora.*

PENDERED, Mary. *The Fair Quaker. Hannah Lightfoot and her Relations with George III*, 1910.

PEPYS, Samuel. *Diary.* (Ed R.C.Latham and W.Matthews.)

PUDNEY, John. *London's Docks*, 1975.

RAE, Julia, From Whitby to Wapping, 1991. Captain Cook, Endeavours, 1997.

ROSE. Millicent.*The East End of London*, 1951.

ROWSE, A.L. *The Tower of London in the History of the Nation.* 1972.

ST JOHN of WAPPING. *Parish Registers.*

ST PETER'S LONDON DOCKS.*Parish Magazine.*

STATUTES OF THE REALM. *27.Henry Vlll Cap 35.& 35 Henry Vlll Cap 9* (The apportionment of Wapping Marsh.) *5 & 6 William & Mary Cap 37.* Establishment of St John of Wapping.*6. George IV Cap 105.* For making wet docks in St Katharine's.

STOW, John. *Survey of the Cities of London and Westminster, 1598 and 1603.* Ed. C.L.Kingsford.

STRYPE John. *Survey of the Cities of London and Westminster Brought down to the present time*, 1722.

THORNBURY, Walter. *Old and New London.*

THRUPP, Sylvia L. *The Merchant Class of Mediaeval London*, 1962.

TRENCH, C.V. *The Royal Malady*, 1964.

VICTORIA COUNTY HISTORY. *London I.p.491* (St Thomas of Acon) *p. 587* (Swan's Nest Hermitage) *Middlesex 1. p 120* (Domesday Book) *p312* (Raine's Schools) *11 pi 14* (Population Tables)

WHITE, T.H. *The Age of Scandal*, 1950.

Other Publications by the History of Wapping Trust

- *Waeppa's People - a History of Wapping* by Madge Darby.
  - A5, softback, 90pp, illustrated - £3.50
  Published 1988 by Conner & Butler - ISBN 0 947699

- *William Peckover of Wapping - Gunner of the Bounty* - by Madge Darby - A5, softback, illustrated, maps 14pp - £1.00
  Published 1989 by Connner & Butler - ISBN 0 947699 12 0

- *Judge Jeffreys and the Ivy Case* - by Madge Darby
  - A5, softback, illustrated, maps, 42pp - £3.00
  Published 1989 by Conner & Butler - ISBN 0 947699 13 9

- *Captain Bligh in Wapping* - by Madge Darby.
  - A5, softback, 18pp, illustrated, map - £1.20
  Pub. 1990 History of Wapping Trust - ISBN 1 873086 00 8

- *Colonel Thomas Rainsborough - Wapping's Most Famous Soldier* by Lincoln S Jones
  Civil War tale - A5, softback, illustrated, map, 18pp - £1.20
  Pub. 1990 by History of Wapping Trust - ISBN 1 873086 03 2

- *The Hermitage Shelter Minutes - December 1940 - an air raid shelter in Hermitage Wharf* edited by Madge Darby - A5, softback, illustrated, map,18pp - £1.20
  Pub. 1990 by History of Wapping Trust - ISBN 1 873086 01 6

- *A Riverside Journey in Picture Postcards - from Tower Bridge to Blackwall Pier* - by Steve Kentfield, Ray Newton - A4, softback, 54pp - £4.95
  Pub. 1990 by History of Wapping Trust - ISBN 1 873086 02 4

- *South of Commercial Road - a photographic record 1934 -1997* - by Ray Newton, John Tarby, Steve Kentfield, Tom Newton
  A4 Softback, 44 pages - £5.95
  Pub. 2001 by History of Wapping Trust - ISBN 1 873086 040